THE SPREAD OF AIDS

Other Books in the At Issue Series:

Affirmative Action
Business Ethics
Domestic Violence
Environmental Justice
Ethnic Conflict
Immigration Policy
The Jury System
Legalizing Drugs
The Media and Politics
The Militia Movement
Policing the Police
Rape on Campus
Single-Parent Families
Smoking
The United Nations
U.S. Policy Toward China
Voting Behavior
Welfare Reform
What Is Sexual Harassment?

THE SPREAD OF AIDS

Daniel A. Leone, *Book Editor*

An Opposing Viewpoints® Series

Greenhaven Press, Inc.
San Diego, California

Library of Congress Cataloging-in-Publication Data

The spread of AIDS / Daniel A. Leone, book editor.
p. cm. — (At issue)
Includes bibliographical references and index.
ISBN 1-56510-537-0 (pbk.) — ISBN 1-56510-538-9 (lib.)
1. AIDS (Disease)—Prevention. I. Leone, Daniel A., 1969– .
II. Series: At Issue (San Diego, Calif.).
RA644.A25S677 1997
362.1'969792—dc20 96-42912
CIP

Printed in the U.S.A.

Table of Contents

Introduction

In June 1981, the U.S. Centers for Disease Control (CDC) published the first reports of a strange disease contracted by five men in Los Angeles. The men suffered from weight loss, high fevers, and pneumocystis, an unusual lung infection. The disease eventually became known as AIDS (acquired immunodeficiency syndrome). Additional investigation and research revealed that this deadly disease was not confined to the United States. It is now believed that HIV (human immunodeficiency virus), the virus that is widely acknowledged to be the cause of AIDS, originated in Central Africa and evolved from a similar virus that has been present in certain monkey populations for over fifty-thousand years. Since its discovery in 1981, the disease has spread dramatically. By the end of 1995, the CDC had reported that the total number of AIDS cases in the United States had grown to 513,486 and that 319,849 of those cases had already resulted in death. The World Health Organization estimates that as many as 40 million people worldwide may become infected with HIV by the beginning of the twenty-first century. If this estimate is accurate, humanity may face one of the most devastating plagues in recorded history.

While the possibility of a cure or vaccine for AIDS remains uncertain, most experts agree that society must rely on other strategies to control the spread of the disease and that these strategies must take into account the atypical process by which people become infected with HIV. Many other infectious diseases are spread through the inhalation or ingestion of, or physical contact with, a virus or bacterium. In contrast, HIV spreads only through the exchange of certain bodily fluids—most commonly, semen and blood. These fluids can be exchanged during a variety of activities. However, the three activities in which they are most commonly passed in amounts large enough to transmit the virus are sex, blood transfusions, and the sharing of needles by intravenous drug users. Health officials have instituted various measures to protect the blood supply and reduce HIV transmission via blood transfusions. However, because sex and needle sharing are typically voluntary actions that are the result of personal decisions, individual behavior is a major factor in the spread of the disease by these means. Consequently, most of the strategies put forth to control the spread of AIDS have focused on changing behavior that places individuals at risk of contracting HIV via sex and needle sharing.

One frequently suggested AIDS prevention strategy is to encourage abstinence from high-risk behaviors. Many commentators argue that the most effective way to avoid HIV infection is to eliminate practices such as promiscuous sexual activity and intravenous drug use. William F. Buckley, a conservative columnist and editor-at-large of the *National Review*, asserts, "Since over 70 percent of those who contract AIDS do so via sex, why does it not make sense, in the course of affirming our dedication to fighting the virus, explicitly to discourage such sexual activity as risks spreading the virus?"

Other AIDS prevention strategists believe that it is unrealistic to expect individuals to abstain from high-risk behavior such as promiscuous sex. They contend that people will continue to be involved in high-risk behavior and, therefore, AIDS prevention strategies should attempt to minimize the risk experienced while engaging in such behavior. Many advocate the use of condoms to reduce the risk of HIV transmission during sexual intercourse. In addition, some public health experts promote safe-sex education and condom distribution programs in schools. They believe that such programs will not only lower the incidence of HIV, but will also provide individuals—and particularly teenagers—with a foundation on which to develop responsible sexual values and the ability to make more informed and intelligent decisions regarding sex.

Opponents of safe-sex education and condom distribution in schools contend that such programs encourage sexual activity and provide a false sense of security about the protection offered by condoms. These critics argue that sex education programs teach teenagers that premarital sex is acceptable and even expected. In addition, many question the effectiveness of condoms in preventing HIV infection. Commentators cite a study published in the *New England Journal of Medicine* that involved married couples in which one partner was HIV-infected and condoms were used regularly. Within two years, 10 percent of the healthy partners had also become infected. In response to such findings, critics of sex education and condom distribution programs contend that sexual abstinence and self-control are the only truly effective solutions for controlling the spread of AIDS.

In addition to attempting to lower the risk of becoming infected with HIV during sex, AIDS prevention strategists also seek to reduce the risks associated with intravenous drug use. To that end, many experts advocate needle-exchange programs, in which addicts are given sterile needles in exchange for their used ones. Proponents argue that needle-exchange programs have proved to be an effective means for controlling HIV infection among addicts. A study conducted by the National Research Council (NRC), a division of the National Academy of Sciences, concluded that needle-exchange programs considerably reduce the spread of AIDS among intravenous drug users and that they do not encourage drug abuse. The authors of the study state that "for injection drug users who cannot or will not stop injecting drugs, the once-only use of sterile needles and syringes remains the safest, most effective approach for limiting HIV transmission." In addition, needle-exchange advocates maintain that by providing assistance and education for addicts through the exchange programs, society sends a positive message and demonstrates compassion for a group of individuals who are usually neglected and ostracized.

Critics question the effectiveness of needle-exchange programs and contend that providing addicts with needles encourages and legitimizes drug abuse. They argue that the success of needle-exchange programs has been exaggerated by their proponents. In addition, opponents insist that even if the programs did reduce the sharing of needles, they would do nothing to slow the spread of HIV from infected addicts to their sexual partners. They believe that the primary factor that leads to the spread of HIV among intravenous drug users is their unwillingness to accept responsibility for their actions. In an article in the *New York Times*, Dr. Mitchell Rosenthal, an expert on drug rehabilitation programs, asserts,

"Indeed, clean needles aren't going to alter any of the irresponsible and antisocial ways in which drug abusers threaten society." Exchange opponents maintain that by supplying addicts with needles, society pushes them further away from treatment, as well as from any hope of ever becoming productive and responsible human beings.

Preventing the spread of AIDS is one of the most formidable and important challenges humanity has ever faced. Opinions among health care professionals, laypersons, religious leaders, and gay rights activists on how to deal with this problem vary greatly, ranging from mandatory AIDS testing to sexual abstinence to the implementation of programs to make high-risk behavior safer. *At Issue: The Spread of AIDS* explores these and other proposed strategies for responding to the complex and controversial issue of AIDS control and prevention.

1

A Global Strategy Is Needed to Control the Spread of AIDS

Jonathan M. Mann and Daniel J.M. Tarantola

Jonathan M. Mann is François-Xavier Bagnoud Professor of Health and Human Rights at Harvard School of Public Health. Daniel J.M. Tarantola is Director of the International AIDS Program at Harvard School of Public Health.

While the AIDS pandemic has aggressively continued its spread, the global response has not increased proportionately and has even declined in some areas. As societies build and develop a new effort to combat the epidemic, an important discovery must be incorporated: There is empirical evidence to support a connection between the risk of HIV infection and the denial of basic human rights. Groups who are marginalized and discriminated against have a greater risk of HIV infection than those whose rights are protected. Therefore, the new global AIDS strategy must include efforts that promote basic human rights for all social groups.

Infection by the Human Immunodeficiency Virus (HIV), the virus that causes Acquired Immune Deficiency Syndrome (AIDS), has been spreading at an alarming rate. The HIV/AIDS crisis has progressively intensified worldwide, yet the global response to the pandemic has plateaued and even declined in many areas. Currently, however, a new UN AIDS program is being launched. This event provides a unique opportunity for serious reflection upon the status of the pandemic and the lessons that have been learned from more than a decade of efforts to confront it. The experience and knowledge that have accumulated worldwide must be transformed into a new, more effective, more coherent global AIDS strategy.

One of the more important discoveries that has emerged from this body of knowledge is that populations which, prior to the arrival of HIV/AIDS, were marginalized, discriminated against, or stigmatized have a higher risk of becoming infected with HIV. Discrimination and societal

Jonathan M. Mann and Daniel J.M. Tarantola, "Preventive Medicine: A Broader Approach to the AIDS Crisis," *Harvard International Review*, vol. 17, no. 4 (Fall 1995), pp. 46-49, 87.

marginalization are evidence of a lack of respect for human rights and human dignity. Therefore, the failure to respect human rights can now be identified as a major cause, or even a root cause, of societal vulnerability to HIV/AIDS. It is now clear that HIV/AIDS is as much about society as it is about a virus. This new understanding of the societal basis for vulnerability to HIV/AIDS has the potential to provide strategic coherence to efforts in HIV/AIDS prevention and control.

The failure to respect human rights can now be identified as a major cause . . . of societal vulnerability to HIV/AIDS.

While the details of the origins and emergence of HIV are unknown, it is clear that the current worldwide epidemic began in the mid-to-late 1970s. By 1980, an estimated 100,000 people worldwide were HIV-infected; this number increased one-hundred-fold during the 1980s, to reach a cumulative total of approximately 10 million people by 1990. The Global AIDS Policy Coalition (GAPC), an independent, international, multidisciplinary organization based at the Harvard School of Public Health estimates that, as of January 1, 1995, 26 million people worldwide were infected with HIV. Of these, about 23 million were adults, including 13.2 million men, 10 million women, and 2.7 million children. The largest number of HIV-infected adults were in sub-Saharan Africa: 17.3 million, about two-thirds of the global total. Overall, over 90 percent of HIV infections have, thus far, occurred in the developing world; only about five percent of HIV-infected people worldwide have been from North America.

The average time between becoming infected with HIV and the onset of clinical AIDS is approximately ten years. Therefore, as the pandemic is a relatively new phenomenon, there are presently many more people infected with HIV than have developed AIDS. The worldwide cumulative total of people with AIDS, as of January 1, 1995, was 8.5 million, of whom seven million were in sub-Saharan Africa, about 700,000 were in Latin America and the Caribbean, and over 550,000 were in North America, Western Europe, and Oceania combined. The estimate of 8.5 million people with AIDS includes 1.9 million children, 92 percent of whom are from sub-Saharan Africa.

Epidemiological trends

The pandemic remains dynamic, volatile, and unstable, and its major impact is yet to come. HIV continues to spread in all already affected areas of the world. It is estimated that in recent years, 40,000 to 80,000 new HIV infections have occurred each year in the United States. While in some areas the rate of increase in the number of people newly infected each year may have slowed, new infections continue to occur; there is no HIV-affected community or country in which HIV transmission has stopped. During 1994 alone, an estimated four million people worldwide became newly infected with HIV, a daily average of nearly 11,000 people;

this is more than the total number of people infected during the entire period between 1975 and 1985.

HIV also continues to spread to countries and communities that were previously unaffected or little affected by the pandemic. For example, while very few people in Asia were HIV-infected prior to the late 1980s, countries such as India, Thailand, and Burma are now experiencing major HIV epidemics and epidemics have begun in other Asian countries, including Malaysia, Nepal, and Vietnam. The cumulative number of HIV-infected people in Southeast Asia, 4.5 million, is now more than twice the total number of HIV-infected people in the entire industrialized world. GAPC estimates that as of 1995, the annual number of new HIV infections in Southeast Asia exceeded the number of infections in sub-Saharan Africa.

Cumulative HIV and AIDS cases worldwide as of January 1, 1995

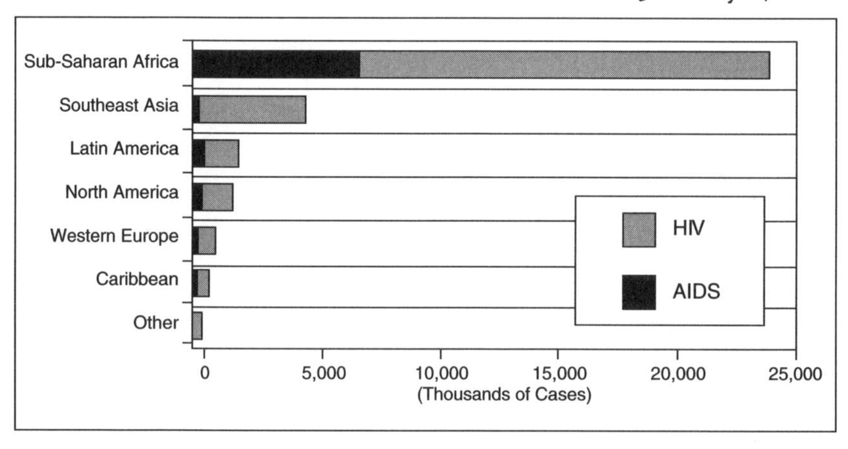

As the pandemic continues to spread and accelerate, it is becoming increasingly more complex. The routes of HIV spread have remained constant and quite limited: sexual intercourse, blood contact, and mother-to-fetus or newborn. However, regardless of where and among whom the epidemic starts in a particular community, the combination of available routes of spread and the long period during which infected people remain potentially capable of transmitting HIV provide it with the capacity to spread within a community in increasingly complex ways. For example, the epidemic in Brazil started among gay men from the social elite, yet it is now centered among heterosexual men and women living in the large slums around Rio de Janeiro and Sao Paolo.

In the United States in 1985, women accounted for about seven percent of AIDS cases; during 1994, 18.1 percent of AIDS cases were women. The proportion of AIDS cases in the United States attributable to intravenous drug use or heterosexual contact has also steadily increased. Therefore, with time, the epidemic in any community becomes a composite of many different smaller epidemics; within large urban areas worldwide, multiple, simultaneous community HIV epidemics are generally underway. Accordingly, the global epidemic must be seen as a composite of all of these individual epidemics.

Due principally to the long average period of about ten years between initial infection with HIV and development of clinical AIDS, the major impact of the pandemic will be delayed. The situation in Thailand illustrates the magnitude of this feature of the HIV/AIDS pandemic. Assuming conservatively that at least 500,000 Thais are HIV-infected, it can be projected that the number of AIDS cases in Thailand will increase from perhaps several hundred between 1990 and 1995 to at least 100,000 between 1995 and 2000. The long period of potential transmissibility combined with the time-lag between HIV infection and onset of disease gives the pandemic tremendous momentum. Even if the spread of HIV stopped immediately, the effects of the pandemic would continue through those who have already been infected.

The impact of AIDS on society

Even a brief review of the status of the HIV/AIDS pandemic must outline the enormous range of societal impacts that it has. Economic impacts of the pandemic include direct health care costs, which are estimated at more than US$11 billion worldwide in 1993. There are also indirect economic costs that result from the loss of productive young adults. In 1994, AIDS became the leading cause of death among 25- to 44-year-olds in the United States. In Thailand, the direct and indirect costs of AIDS during the 1990s were estimated at US$8 billion, not including the probable decline in tourism, which is currently a US$5 billion industry, or the decline in foreign investment because of the prevalence of the disease.

At a more individual and household level, the consequences of HIV/AIDS are diverse and profound. In large part, this stems from the disproportionate concentration of HIV infection and mortality among young and middle-aged adults. Few diseases other than AIDS target these age groups, and the deaths of these people mean the loss of mothers and fathers, active workers, and supporters of families. HIV/AIDS is a disease affecting many families. For example, by 2000, there will be an estimated 220,000 to 300,000 AIDS orphans in the Ivory Coast, 380,000 to 580,000 AIDS orphans in Kenya, and from 70,000 to 125,000 AIDS orphans in the United States.

HIV/AIDS has often provoked serious expressions of discrimination.

In Tanzania, affected households spend an average of one year's per capita income on care and funerals—two-thirds of this expenditure for the funeral alone. The loss of adult workers also has a transgenerational effect as the children in an affected household are less likely to attend school. Even in industrialized countries, the economic impacts of HIV/AIDS are substantial. For example, in Canada in 1994, estimated production losses due to HIV/AIDS amounted to more than ten percent of market output among men aged 25 to 64 years old. From 1987 to 1991, the average production loss per death for Canadian men was US$558,000, more than for any other cause of death. Similarly, in the United States in 1991, estimated foregone earnings associated with AIDS deaths was US$28 billion to US$36 billion.

In addition to economic and family dislocation, HIV/AIDS has often provoked serious expressions of discrimination and stigmatization. Public policy debates are often dominated by fear and demagoguery. For example, the US Congress refused to drop restrictions on the entry of HIV-infected people into the United States despite the unanimous opinion of public health experts that such rules have little or no impact on the epidemic and, in fact, mislead US residents into thinking that the HIV threat is an "outside" one. Issues such as mandatory testing, reporting, and even, in the case of Cuba, mandatory isolation of HIV-infected people, continue to arise despite the World Health Organization's (WHO's) clear statement that discrimination and coercion are counter-productive to efforts to prevent and control HIV infection.

The global response: A history

The history of the global response to HIV/AIDS can be divided into four periods. During the first period, from the mid-1970s until 1981, there was no response, for the pandemic was spreading silently and unnoticed. Then, from 1981, when AIDS was first recognized, until 1985, enormous amounts of scientific knowledge were accumulated. Yet, during this period of discovery and initial response, there was little public health awareness or action. Nearly all of the important work in HIV prevention during this period was carried out by community organizations or non-governmental organizations (NGOs). Few governments became actively involved in HIV/AIDS prevention, and no international organizations targeted HIV/AIDS for particular attention.

Finally, in the mid 1980s, AIDS was recognized to be a global threat, affecting both the industrialized and developing world. WHO launched a major effort, catalyzing a global mobilization, from 1986 to 1990. During this time a global AIDS strategy was created, national AIDS programs were developed in most countries, and community-based efforts were further expanded and intensified. The speed, intensity, and scope of this mobilization to confront this truly global health problem was unprecedented.

While the AIDS effort became the largest component of WHO and as resources committed to confronting the pandemic in the developing world increased dramatically from less than US$1 million in 1986 to over US$200 million in 1990, the major challenge became developing a coherent analysis of and approach to controlling the pandemic. In 1986, WHO developed the Global AIDS Strategy, which arguably can be considered the world's first truly global strategy in the fight against AIDS. The Global AIDS Strategy encouraged each country to develop its own comprehensive national AIDS program based on a common understanding of the basis for effective prevention programs. WHO then worked to assure human and financial resources and technical support for the implementation of prevention programs in each country.

Prevention was based on three vital components, two of which were drawn from the traditional vocabulary of public health, while the third was strikingly original. The first element was an information and education campaign, which had to be developed with the participation of its intended audience. However, knowledge about HIV/AIDS was not enough, therefore the second element involved health and social services, which were closely linked with prevention messages. For example, information about condom use had to be accompanied by programs to ensure that condoms were readily available, affordable, and of good quality. Similarly, recommendations about HIV testing were only meaningful where confidential counseling and high-quality testing services were available.

The third key element of successful HIV prevention—preventing discrimination against HIV-infected people and people with AIDS—was highly innovative in public health terms. The rationale for antidiscrimination emerged from field experiences, through which it became evident that when those most likely to be HIV-infected were threatened with severe social consequences, such as loss of work, inability to marry, or expulsion from school, they would "go underground" to avoid contact with the public health system. Thus, societal support for infected and ill people was identified to be just as important for successful prevention as information or health services.

When this "prevention triad" was applied and adapted to local cultural and other circumstances, it was highly effective. Whether for homosexual men, commercial sex users, intravenous drug users, adolescents, or heterosexual men and women, the Global AIDS Strategy's approach proved to be as successful, or more so, than any other public health program seeking to change individual behavior.

Despite the global mobilization and successful prevention programs at the pilot project and community level, the fourth and most recent period in the history of HIV/AIDS, from 1990 to present, has been deeply disappointing.

However, despite the global mobilization and successful prevention programs at the pilot project and community level, the fourth and most recent period in the history of HIV/AIDS, from 1990 to present, has been deeply disappointing. Unfortunately, while the global epidemic has intensified and expanded, the global response has stagnated or even declined. Successful pilot projects have not been replicated. The gap between the rich and poor widens, as currently about 90 percent of resources for prevention and care are spent in the industrialized world, while the developing world bears about 90 percent of the HIV/AIDS burden. The political and social commitment to fight HIV/AIDS has not kept pace with the pandemic. Because the WHO Global AIDS Strategy failed to evolve and develop based upon its experiences, the current period has been characterized by confusion, fragmentation of efforts, and inaction.

Despite the increasing gap between the pace of the pandemic and the global response, it is now possible to revitalize and rekindle global, national, and community efforts. This opportunity derives from a recent discovery about the pandemic. Study of the evolving epidemic in countries around the world has uncovered a powerful and previously unrecognized risk factor for HIV infection at a societal level. Populations that are marginalized, stigmatized, and discriminated against are at higher risk of infection. For example, in the United States, the epidemic is increasingly concentrated in inner-city and poor African-American and Latino populations.

In another example, it is now considered a risk factor for women in East Africa to be married and monogamous. Even if a woman knows that her husband is HIV-infected, she cannot refuse unwanted or unprotected sexual intercourse, for fear of being beaten without civil recourse or for fear of divorce, which effectively results in social and economic death for the woman. Therefore, despite knowledge about HIV/AIDS and despite the availability of condoms in the marketplace, these women cannot protect themselves. They lack the equal rights that alone would enable the translation of knowledge into protection. Efforts to change the laws governing divorce, marriage, and inheritance are now underway—as part of a broad strategy to slow the spread of HIV.

Emergence of a new global AIDS strategy

The discovery of this connection between marginalization and vulnerability to infection provides potential strategic coherence to efforts in HIV/AIDS prevention and control. The lack of acknowledgment and respect for human rights demonstrated by the existence of discrimination and stigmatization is almost certainly a major risk factor for HIV-infection. Indeed, it may be argued that the existence of such marginalizing conditions is the most important risk factor. It is essential to emphasize that this understanding emerged through concrete and practical experience, not from simple theoretical considerations; it was discovered in communities, not in governmental bureaucracies or universities. This phenomenon has been empirically proven, and it indicates that the AIDS problem is part and parcel of broader social problems.

This insight regarding the inextricable connection between the promotion and protection of health and the promotion and protection of human rights offers a new avenue for work against HIV/AIDS. It suggests that a two-pronged strategy is now needed. The first part of such a strategy would involve an effort to strengthen existing programs around the world that are based upon the "prevention triad" concepts. These efforts require and deserve continued support at the community, national, and global levels.

The lack of acknowledgment and respect for human rights . . . is almost certainly a major risk factor for HIV-infection.

The second, truly innovative, part of such a new global AIDS strategy would require that the societal roots of the pandemic be addressed directly. This will require a commitment, within each society, to promoting and protecting the basic human rights of people currently marginalized and discriminated against. This effort may initially seem unusual for or beyond the scope of public health. Yet public health has been defined as "ensuring the conditions in which people can be healthy"—and the major determinants of health status are societal. Therefore, concrete efforts to help transform society by promoting increased respect for human rights can be understood as a vital way to help ensure the "essential conditions" both for HIV prevention and for health more generally.

The challenge today is to convert this critical insight into the societal dimensions of vulnerability to HIV/AIDS into policy. Yet, since how a problem is defined determines what is done about it, this new understanding of the pandemic and its central dynamic is the most important and potentially useful lesson derived from over a decade of work against HIV/AIDS. Hope arises also from the recognition by the United Nations that a truly coordinated global effort is required to confront the diverse challenges of HIV/AIDS prevention and care. Starting in January 1996, a new Joint and Co-Sponsored UN AIDS program will exist. This program will link together the six major UN agencies involved with HIV/AIDS: WHO, the UN Children's Fund, the UN Development Programme, The UN Educational, Scientific, and Cultural Organization, the UN Fund for Population, and the World Bank.

A global village in every sense

Projections for the HIV/AIDS pandemic are grim. While estimates for the number of people HIV-infected by the year 2000 vary widely—from 40 to 110 million people worldwide—it is clear that the years to come will be much more difficult than the nearly 15 years since AIDS was first recognized. Even as new insights, strategies, and programs are developed against HIV/AIDS, the experience of this pandemic serves as a warning for the future. For today's world is more vulnerable than ever before to the global spread of new and emerging diseases. The extraordinary and dramatic increase in the movement of people, goods, and ideas worldwide has truly made this world a "global village." Therefore, whether it involves old diseases or previously unrecognized pathogens, it is merely a matter of when, not a matter of if, the next global epidemic will occur.

Aside from a new understanding of the inextricable connection between health and human rights—which applies to all major health problems of the modern world, including cancer, heart disease, injuries, violence, and infectious diseases—perhaps the most important lesson to be learned from the "age of AIDS" is the message of global interdependence. For we can no longer believe that our borders will protect us; the health of the world is bound together. In order to respond to this phenomenon, the basis of our approach to the world's health will have to be reconsidered. It will be necessary to view every disease and epidemic as a potentially global phenomenon. It will also be necessary to evaluate health concerns within the larger context of societal conditions and circumstances. WHO may literally have to be re-invented, and the shape of our future may be in the balance.

2

AIDS Prevention and Treatment Strategies Should Target the Third World

Robert Vitillo

Robert Vitillo, a priest of the Diocese of Paterson, New Jersey, is head of programs at Caritas Internationalis, the umbrella organization for Catholic development and relief agencies. He presented the following viewpoint at a meeting of the Vatican of Catholic development and relief officials.

The AIDS pandemic is a global problem. While the industrialized world has suffered an increasing number of AIDS cases, over 90 percent of cases are found in developing nations. Since 1990, HIV infection rates have soared in Asian countries such as India and Thailand. Young women in these areas are particularly susceptible. Despite this disproportionate impact on developing nations, however, less than 10 percent of the total worldwide funding for AIDS prevention programs and research is expended in Third World countries. In order to control the spread of AIDS, more funding needs to be directed toward these regions of the world.

In Australasia, North America and Western Europe, human immunodeficiency virus, or HIV, first spread widely during the late 1970s and early 1980s. The groups most affected are homosexual and bisexual men and injecting drug users, but infection among heterosexuals is rapidly increasing. In North America, the men-to-women ratio of AIDS cases has halved, from 14-to-1 in 1984 to 7-to-1 in 1993. The World Health Organization estimates the following number of infections in the respective regions:

- Australasia: 25,000 HIV infections.
- North America: 1 million HIV infections.
- Western Europe: 500,000 HIV infections.

In Latin America, HIV first spread in the early 1980s among homosexual and bisexual men, and among injecting drug users; infection rates

Robert Vitillo, "The Expanding Global AIDS Pandemic," *Origins*, vol. 24, no. 37 (March 2, 1995).

of 20 percent to 76 percent have been recorded among injecting drug users in Brazil. But heterosexual intercourse is now the leading mode of transmission; infection rates are increasing rapidly among women, as is mother-to-child transmission. In the Caribbean, heterosexual transmission is now well established, and the men-to-women ratio is 1.5-to-1. WHO estimates that 2 million infections have occurred in Latin America and the Caribbean.

In sub-Saharan Africa, extensive spread of HIV probably started in the 1970s, and the major factor in transmission has been heterosexual intercourse. This region has 10 percent of the world's population, but accounts for two out of every three HIV infections among adults, over 80 percent of infections among women worldwide and 90 percent of infections among infants. It is the only region of the world where there are more women infected than men: 11 to 12 women for every 10 men. WHO estimates that more than 10 million people (including nearly 1 million children) have been infected with HIV in sub-Saharan Africa.

Among the populations of North Africa and the Middle East, very little information is available on the incidence of HIV infection and of AIDS. Heterosexual intercourse and injecting drug use are believed to be the main modes of transmission, although sex between men may also play a part. Reports have suggested a high number of cases of sexually transmitted diseases in the region, and there is evidence of a substantial trade in heroin and other drugs in the area. HIV levels are rising—in Djibouti, for example, 4 percent of women seeking antenatal care are HIV infected. WHO estimates that the region may have more than 100,000 cumulative HIV infections.

AIDS around the world

A 60 percent increase in the number of reported cases of AIDS occurred during 1994. More than 1 million cases of AIDS have been reported to WHO; it is estimated that there are at least 4 million cases worldwide. By the year 2000, the cumulative number of cases is at least expected to double and may reach 10 million.

Asia now accounts for 6 percent of the global total; this represents an eightfold increase in a one-year period. In Chiang Mai, Thailand; Bombay, India; and Yandoon, Burma, an obvious impact on health care services has already been noted.

In Masaka, Uganda, 50 percent of all deaths are AIDS-related. Ninety percent of deaths in the 25-to-40-year-old population are AIDS-related in this same area. This has caused a serious impact on labor and commercial sectors and has required an increase in costs for training new staff.

Marked increase of HIV infection in Asia:

- From 2 percent to 54 percent among commercial sex workers in Bombay between 1984 and 1992.
- From 2 percent to 55 percent among injecting drug users in Manipur state, India, between 1989 and 1990.
- Tenfold increase among blood donors in Cambodia (0.076 percent to 0.75 percent) in a one-year period (1991–1992).
- Threefold increase among blood donors in Malaysia (11 percent to 30 percent) from 1991–1992.

- Among foreign hospitality girls in Japan, the HIV-seroprevalence rate is 2 percent to 6 percent. In Singapore, Malaysians make up 92.7 percent of commercial sex workers and account for sexually transmitted disease incidences of 45 to 60 per 100. More than 20,000 Nepali girls work in Bombay brothels, up to 30 percent of whom could be HIV-infected.
- The link between tuberculosis and HIV is already being seen in India, Vietnam and the Philippines (where tuberculosis occurs in more than 60 percent of persons with AIDS). In Chiang Mai, HIV coinfection with TB increased from 5.4 percent in 1989 to 20.6 percent in 1992.

The evolution of the pandemic is accelerating in South and Southeast Asia where it is thought that HIV only began to spread in the mid-1980s or later. Although HIV first appeared among injecting drug users and homosexual men, and infected, unscreened blood (to be used for transfusions and administration of blood products) is a serious problem in some countries (India, for example), heterosexual transmission is now dominant.

The epidemic has been growing at a pace which is reminiscent of that in sub-Saharan Africa in the early 1980s, but may have an even greater potential for spread in the world's most populous region (India alone has a larger population than the whole of the African continent). Estimated infections in Thailand have risen tenfold since early 1990; in India, they have tripled since 1992. WHO estimates that 2.5 million people have already been infected in this region—1 million more than in July 1993.

HIV spread through East Asia and the Pacific from the mid-1980s, but there is limited data available for the most populated country in the region, China. With regard to China, the infection has been found near the Burmese border among injecting drug users and is spreading there in epidemic proportions; it has also been found in the provinces adjacent to Hong Kong. HIV is transmitted sexually as well as through injecting drug use in this region, and most of the small island countries and territories of the Pacific have reported at least one case of AIDS. WHO estimates that more than 50,000 HIV infections have occurred in the region.

At least 90 percent of the cases of HIV/AIDS are found in the developing world.

In Eastern Europe and the former Soviet Union, major social and political upheavals in the last few years have increased the potential for the spread of HIV within and across communities. The following risk factors for the spread of HIV can be found in all the countries of this region:

- Mass migrations following the opening of borders.
- Economic hardship linked to market reforms.
- Civil conflicts.

Among the most affected groups in this region are homosexual men and injecting drug users. There have been recorded incidents in Romania and the former Soviet Union of transmission of HIV to children in hospital and institutional settings through use of unsterilized equipment and unscreened blood transfusions. WHO estimates that there may be more than 50,000 HIV infections in the area, but warns that this figure may be misleading due to lack of accurate data.

Cost of prevention and care

WHO estimates that key HIV-prevention programs could be implemented successfully in developing countries for between $1.5 billion and $2.9 billion per year. This represents only one-twentieth of the amount spent on Operation Desert Storm, which cost the sum of $49 billion during a several-week period.

It is estimated that implementation of basic prevention programs in Asia would cost between $770 million and $1.5 billion a year. This represents less than 0.03% of Asia's economic output—or, to put it another way, the equivalent of what Japan's workers produce in less than one hour. An investment of this kind could save an estimated 5 million infections by the year 2000 alone.

When taking into account the meager funds which are expended on HIV/AIDS services, we are confronted once again with many inequities. Thus we note that during 1992, 80 percent of HIV-infected people lived in developing countries, while 95 percent of the $7 billion spent on AIDS education, care and research was expended in the industrialized world.

Impact on women

Up to 60 percent of all infections occurring in women take place before 20 years of age. Young women between 15 to 19 years of age are four times more likely to be HIV-infected than their male counterparts.

Gender inequality gives less control to women:

- Women often are forced to be sexually active at an early age.
- Sugar daddies seek out young women as "safe" partners.
- One-twentieth of teen-agers worldwide are suffering from sexually transmitted diseases.
- Anal intercourse is commonly practiced in attempts to avoid pregnancy.
- Female genital mutilation is a common practice in many parts of Africa and the Middle East. Between 85 million to 114 million women have endured this worldwide, and it often occurs between the ages of 4 and 8 years. These women are often subjected to anal intercourse because vaginal intercourse is not possible.
- Young women are often deprived of formal education and thus do not benefit from regular channels of communication and education about HIV prevention.
- Poverty and miserable conditions often deprive young women of minimal privacy and expose them to abuse, often from family members.
- Girls who have been raped are made outcasts by their families and local communities, and thus are often forced to sell themselves in order to survive on the streets.
- Development, which raises socioeconomic conditions and reduces dependence on migration and prostitution, can limit the spread of HIV/AIDS.

Perhaps these issues are best summarized by the word of the secretary general of the United Nations, Dr. Boutros Boutros-Ghali, to the AIDS summit meeting which was held in Paris on World AIDS Day, Dec. 1, 1994:

> Fifty years ago, the United Nations organization was created to fight war and underdevelopment. Today we are well aware of the link between peace and development. Without peace, there can be no lasting development. Without development, there can be no true peace.
>
> So our action to combat AIDS must be viewed in that light. We must be under no illusion that the struggle against AIDS is part and parcel of the worldwide struggle of the international community for world security. When we say no to AIDS—just as we say no to war and underdevelopment—we are declaring collectively that AIDS is neither inevitable nor unconquerable; that humankind will in time rise above this new and murderous challenge; and that the entire international community must now mobilize its efforts for the fight for life.

Key issues

- At least 90 percent of the cases of HIV/AIDS are found in the developing world; the people most at risk are the poorest.
- Every day approximately 6,000 people become newly infected with HIV.
- Ninety-two percent of the estimated $14.2 billion annual spending on HIV/AIDS prevention and care is spent in the industrialized world.
- High and rising rates of sexually transmitted diseases, which remain untreated because of inadequate health care, increase vulnerability to HIV and are thought to be responsible for much of the explosive spread of the virus in the developing world.
- Forty percent of the HIV-infected adults today are women; in 1990, women accounted only for 25 percent of adult infections.
- Because so many women are financially or socially dependent upon men, they rarely have the power to protect themselves from infection.
- HIV/AIDS is both a symptom and increasingly a cause of underdevelopment.

By the year 2000, WHO estimates that as many as 40 million people may have become infected with HIV worldwide; other expert and reliable sources estimate that the actual total may be greater than 100 million.

Among these, it is expected that:

- Ninety percent of HIV-infected people will be living in developing countries.
- Twenty-five percent will be children.
- Eighty percent of HIV infections will have resulted from heterosexual transmission.
- Up to 10 million people will have been diagnosed with AIDS.
- Ten million children will have been orphaned as a result of the death to AIDS among one or both parents.

Conclusions

1. Consciousness-raising efforts have been successful within the confederation [the network of Catholic development and relief agencies] but must continue especially among hierarchy and other religious and lay leaders; church-related health care workers; church-related development workers.

2. Emergency-aid funding will be necessary to strengthen health care responses to those already suffering from AIDS; priority should be given to home care and primary care-oriented services.

3. Much emphasis is needed on effective prevention and behavior-change programs, especially for youth.

4. We need to link HIV/AIDS response to other Caritas education, development and human-promotion programs (e.g., linkage of HIV/AIDS education with child nutrition programs in the Philippines).

5. After raising consciousness among Caritas organizations in certain regions, the network must be ready to respond by sharing expertise and resources (e.g., problems with response to project proposals coming from Latin America).

3

AIDS Treatments Will Not Be Accessible to Third World AIDS Victims

The Economist

The Economist *is Britain's leading newsweekly.*

Researchers have produced a multi-drug therapy for AIDS that holds promise as a potential cure for the disease. However, because of the tremendous cost of the treatment, the Third World will not be able to make it available to its AIDS victims. If driven to do so, the rich countries could export AIDS treatments to poor nations. However, such an effort would not be economically feasible and is therefore not likely to be undertaken.

Mercutio's horrific curse on the warring family clans of Romeo and Juliet—"A plague on both your houses"—carries little terror for today's audiences. In Elizabethan England, the threat of plague was ever present. In the world's rich, developed countries it is now but a distant memory. It has been abolished by better nutrition and sanitation, and the relentless assault of the antibiotics and vaccines developed by modern scientific medicine.

With one exception. For the past 15 years AIDS—acquired immunodeficiency syndrome—has been stalking the auditorium. So far HIV, the virus believed to cause the disease, is reckoned to have destroyed the immune systems of 7 million people across the world. Of those, 4.5 million already have died—succumbing to opportunistic infections such as tuberculosis that a healthy immune system would have fought off. Almost another 19 million people harbor the virus without having, as yet, developed the symptoms of AIDS. And, if the United Nations is to be believed, another 11 million to 14 million people will pick up the virus by 2000.

Until recently, science has looked helpless against this disease. But lately a glimmer of hope has flashed. A series of clinical trials of a new multiple-drug therapy suggests that an effective treatment for AIDS may be near at hand. By putting a new type of drug, known as a protease blocker, into a molecular cocktail with more familiar medicines such as AZT, AIDS researchers have devised a mixture that can suppress the virus far more effectively than before, and to which, they hope, it cannot evolve resistance.

The scientists are not yet talking of a cure. It is too early to be sure whether the treatment will work indefinitely if it is maintained, let alone whether patients will continue to be well if it is withdrawn. But that one word—"well"—is what distinguishes this approach from previous attempts to deal with HIV. People on the new regime of treatment, even some who were probably close to dying, are now recovering the appearance and feeling of health.

If it is confirmed by longer and larger clinical trials, this will rightly be hailed as a scientific triumph. For researchers to have unravelled the mysteries of a novel, lethal infectious disease within a decade and a half, and to have produced a treatment, would be a remarkable feat. The tragedy is that such a victory would not, in itself mark the conquest of AIDS. Indeed, for most of the 21 million or so people carrying HIV, the hope the treatment brings is likely to be the hope of Tantalus: ever present, but out of reach. And that is going to confront the world with a painful moral dilemma.

The reason is price. A year's course of the new therapy is expected to cost over $10,000, and nine out of ten people who contract AIDS live in countries where $10,000 a year exceeds by many times the gross domestic product per head. The medicine's price will no doubt fall as manufacturing technology improves and economies of scale come into play. Competition between drug companies, and new products, should also drive prices lower (three protease blockers already have been approved by America's Food and Drug Administration, and another four are undergoing trials). But this sort of drug therapy is unlikely ever to be cheap.

The new therapy is expected to cost over $10,000.

As a result, the rejoicing that will accompany any confirmation that the new therapy really does work is plainly going to be followed at once by the same mixture of fear, anger and guilt that has become familiar to people who have followed the progress of this cruel epidemic from the start. Can the rich world stomach the spectacle of its own AIDS victims receiving effective treatment while their poorer foreign brethren are left without hope? And what of the drug companies? They will rightly seek to profit from the huge investment they have made in AIDS research, even if this entails setting a price that is higher than most victims will be able to afford. It is safe to assume that there will once again be an outcry against the "excessive" profits of the drug industry as a whole, just as there was when Britain's Wellcome brought its AZT treatment to market just over a decade ago.

To accusations of callousness, the drug industry will trot out its usual defense, namely that without the chance of turning a profit, it would not be able to invest in research for new medicines. When measured against the suffering of people infected with a lethal disease, this point sounds abstract, even callous. The difficulty is that it is true. Governments can do a few things to help make drugs more affordable—for example by ensuring that competition in the industry is as open as possible—but a mindless attack on the industry's profit incentive is a prescription for fewer new medicines in the future.

Can the rich world stomach the spectacle of its own AIDS victims receiving effective treatment while their poorer foreign brethren are left without hope?

Does it then follow that the rich must save themselves and leave the poor to their fate? In theory, if their conscience so dictated, the rich countries could help the poor without damaging the incentives of the drug companies at all. They could simply ship the necessary drugs to sick people in the poor world as part of their overall foreign aid effort. But a glance at the arithmetic—$10,000 multiplied by 20 million—shows how unimaginable this really is. And it is anyway far from obvious that a massive transfer of resources from rich to poor should concentrate on this particular disease.

In the tropics, for example, malaria is by far a bigger killer. In 1990, about $1 billion was spent by governments on AIDS research (most of it by America, whose National Institutes for Health will, this year alone, spend almost $1.5 billion). Yet on malaria only $60 million was spent although, in terms of the disability and premature death that malaria causes, it was then three times as devastating as AIDS. If saving lives is your aim, providing clean water should be a higher priority still.

The wretched upshot is this: that countries choose their priorities in medical research, as in just about everything else, on the basis of their selfish preoccupations. In the United States, powerful lobbying by gay people helped to mobilize a massive scientific campaign against AIDS, which may be about to bear fruit. That is wonderful news.

Because of the prominence of this disease in their own countries, Americans and Europeans will feel a special appalled sympathy for Africans and others who will continue to succumb to it even after a cure has been discovered. Perhaps that will encourage a less parochial attitude toward medical research in the future: AIDS already has changed many attitudes. But that hope seems pretty forlorn.

4

Governments Should Combat the Spread of AIDS

Tim Unsworth

Tim Unsworth, a freelance writer in Chicago, is the author of several books.

The majority of AIDS victims are found among the poor and other disadvantaged social groups. Government and the upper classes, who have demonstrated little concern over the plight of these groups, have not made the necessary commitment to control the AIDS pandemic and have either failed to recognize or have ignored its seriousness. The first step towards eliminating this deadly problem is full acknowledgment of its scope and magnitude. Only then can an appropriate response be undertaken.

I looked and there was a pale green horse. Its rider was named death, and Hades accompanied him. They were given authority over a quarter of the earth, to kill with sword, famine, and plague, and by means of the beasts of the earth.
—Revelation 6:8

Former late-night talk-show host Arsenio Hall liked to poke fun, but he didn't joke about AIDS. He called it "World War III."

He may not be exaggerating.

One of the by-products of the present AIDS epidemic is the potential for the disease—or rather the vaccine to prevent it—to become a kind of medical nuclear weapon. Most authorities agree that a vaccine could be developed by the year 2000. Given the present direction of both economic and scientific intelligence, there is a strong possibility that the U.S. will be the first nation to find a vaccine, just as the country developed and dropped the first atomic bomb in 1945.

At the annual international conference on AIDS held in Amsterdam, Netherlands, in 1992, speaker after speaker raised the specter of a single nation holding the vaccine bottle over poor, underdeveloped countries and demanding concessions in return for the immunizing potion. Even industrialized nations could be held political prisoners.

The international disputes between France and the U.S. over experi-

Tim Unsworth, "How an Epidemic of Fear Fueled an Epidemic of AIDS," *Salt of the Earth*, February 1994. Reprinted with permission from *Salt of the Earth* magazine, published by Claretian Publications, 205 W. Monroe St., Chicago, IL 60606; 1-800-328-6515.

mental vaccines are just one example of the potential for conflict. Some worry that in the future the U.S. may threaten, for example, to withhold a vaccine from an African nation with high rates of HIV infections if it doesn't bow to U.S. economic interests.

A need for concern and compassion

"The social-justice issues are enormous," says Father Robert Rybicki, executive director of Bonaventure House, a residence for terminally ill AIDS patients in Chicago. "We need to realize that there must be a partnership. Who will distribute the vaccine? Maybe the World Health Organization (WHO). Who will pay for it?

"We already have a two-speed disease. Once victims have full-blown AIDS, those in the U.S. live about 20 months. Someone with AIDS in the sub-Sahara will live only six months.

"Collective prevention appears to be giving way to an attitude of 'everyone for him- or herself,'" Rybicki warns. "There is an acceleration of AIDS among the poorer countries. Yet this doesn't appear to carry any urgency nor collective implication for the middle class or the rich. We seem to accept the losses among the poor, the homeless, and the disadvantaged."

Nancy McKenzie, editor of *The Aids Reader*, writes: "Sick people need a stable environment, relevant information, and ultimately, a permanent continuum of health-care resources. Sick people who are also *poor* people spend most of their waking energy trying to procure one or all three."

At the Amsterdam conference it was noted that moralizers often are the concerned people's worst enemies.

Because AIDS in the U.S. has been linked to homosexual activity, many church groups have been preoccupied with blaming the victims for their predicament rather than extending care and joining the fight against the disease.

Fundamentalist political-action groups, for example, have gathered at AIDS rallies and taunted, "You're all going to hell!" AIDS has been an affront to religious conservatives.

The history of the virus could be said to date back virtually to the beginnings of the human race.

Prevention of AIDS is made more difficult by cultural as well as religious barriers. For example, women in some countries die of AIDS before they are even diagnosed. They simply aren't considered important enough to qualify for medical attention. Even U.S. doctors are slow to respond to the increase of AIDS cases among women, many of whom will pass the disease on to their children.

Poverty drives women to prostitution, which exposes them to AIDS. In Thailand, for example, a check of an entire colony of prostitutes revealed that 100 percent were HIV-positive.

According to recent WHO estimates, almost 14 million people worldwide—one out of every 250 adults—are HIV-positive. In sub-Saharan Africa, one out of every 40 adults is infected, and that rate is rising rapidly.

WHO projects that at least 30 million people around the world—10 million of them children—will be infected by the year 2000. Other experts think the number could reach 110 million.

In developing countries, testing for AIDS is virtually nonexistent. WHO is currently exploring ways of bulk-buying and distributing tests to make them less costly.

A history of HIV and AIDS

Despite dogged detective work by the world's best researchers, AIDS (Acquired Immunodeficiency Syndrome) remains one of the most mysterious maladies ever to confront medical science. According to Christine Gorman, correspondent for *Time* magazine, "the more researchers learn about the disease, the more questions they have."

The Human Immunodeficiency Virus (HIV), proclaimed to be the cause of AIDS, has proved to be a fiendishly fast-moving target, able to mutate its structure to elude detection, drugs, and vaccines. No one knows for sure how HIV destroys the human immune system, and puzzled experts have debated whether the virus is the only culprit at work.

The history of the virus could be said to date back virtually to the beginnings of the human race. Microscopic protozoa, especially the organism known as *Pneumocystis carinii,* have found a warm home within the 300 million air sacs in the human body where oxygen from inhaled breath eases into the bloodstream as part of the body's basic fueling process.

In 1910, a Brazilian scientist discovered the protozoa in guinea pigs. Three years later, France's Pasteur Institute found it living quite comfortably in the lungs of Paris sewer rats. It was not until 1942 that it was discovered in people. Further research showed that the insidious creature traced its heritage directly to the most primitive one-celled animals from which all life evolved. It was thought, however, to be just one of tens of thousands of creatures that are easily held in check by the body's normally functioning immune system. These creatures could be said to live on the fringes of biological society. They could break out among poor children living in desperate poverty or cause the rejection of heart transplants at first-rate hospitals.

The early discoveries of *Pneumocystis carinii* became mere footnotes in the vast literature of protozoa. Until 1980, cases involving *Pneumocystis carinii* pneumonia were so rare that they were not connected. In fact, for a brief period after the breakout of AIDS, no connection was made between the disease and the homosexual community.

Another form of the disease, Kaposi's Sarcoma (KS) is a cancer first discovered in 1871 among Mediterranean and Jewish men in the fifth or sixth decade of their lives. It was found in much larger numbers in Africa in 1914, where KS surfaced in one of ten cancer cases.

More recent developments

In 1979, a New York schoolteacher named Rick Wellikoff visited a doctor for blood studies. His condition was later diagnosed as Kaposi's Sarcoma. He had never been to Africa nor did he exhibit the telltale signs of KS—but he was gay.

Homosexuals have been hit by tide after tide of infections—venereal diseases, Hepatitis A and B, and others. In San Francisco, about 80 percent of the clients at the city's VD clinic are gay men. What proved especially insidious with AIDS was the lengthy latency period between infection and outbreak—a period during which sexually active carriers spread the disease.

By mid 1980, the medical community became convinced that a new disease was going around among homosexual men.

Now the disease has crossed many barriers and is frequently transmitted by heterosexual contact, drug use, and blood transfusions.

For a long time, government officials were stuck in a state of denial.

By 1983, the Pasteur Institute reported that it had found the virus linked to AIDS. A year later, the U.S. National Cancer Institute announced that it had isolated the AIDS virus. Those announcements seemed to promise a speedy medical solution for the crisis, but the virus appears to have taken still other directions. In 1987, the U.S. Food and Drug Administration (FDA) approved the experimental use of AZT, the first drug shown to fight AIDS. Since then, however, the value of AZT has come into question.

The death of film star Rock Hudson in 1985 helped to bring the disease to the evening news, as did the death five years later of 18-year-old hemophiliac Ryan White, spurring a U.S. congressional movement to provide funds to cities hit hardest by the disease.

In 1991 the FDA approved a second anti-AIDS drug, DDI, and in 1992 a third one, DDC. But the decade of death continued into the 1990s.

Scientists are still working on a vaccine that will jumpstart the immune system in those already infected as well as on an antivirus that prevents the start of AIDS. The disease, however, evades them. While in the U.S. gay men and drug users still make up the majority of victims, AIDS is becoming a largely heterosexual infection in Africa and Thailand.

In addition, a disturbing number of people with AIDS are developing a deadlier form of tuberculosis than was previously known. It can be spread by simply breathing. It means that more AIDS patients will be quarantined, raising a host of other social and legal problems. Cuba presently isolates all known AIDS victims, ignoring their rights but virtually halting the disease.

A lack of government commitment

Sadly, according to AIDS advocates, governments around the world are slow to respond to the challenge.

A Harvard study has shown that in the U.S. only about $2.70 per person was spent on AIDS prevention in 1992—about the cost of a bottle of vitamin pills. (In the sub-Sahara, this figure dwindles to 7 cents per person.)

AIDS will kill 1 percent of the world's population by the year 2000, more than all who died in World War I.

June Osborn of the U.S. AIDS Commission observes: "This epidemic is of historic scale, but the response has been far short of historic."

In 1987, President Ronald Reagan gave one of his polished speeches before the American Foundation for AIDS Research during which he declared AIDS to be his administration's number-one health priority. But there was little action to back up such rhetoric.

The $50 million the government was spending that year in support of AIDS research represented only about one tenth the cost of a single black-winged Stealth bomber and an infinitesimal slice of a total budget that was approaching $1 trillion.

That was unfortunate, because a few more dollars at the right time could have made a big difference in preventing the spread of AIDS. Dr. Mathilde Krim, co-chair of the American Foundation of AIDS Research, observes, "Everything about this epidemic has been utterly predictable from the very first day. But no one would listen. We definitely could have contained it."

For a long time, government officials were stuck in a state of denial.

"I have not seen enough evidence that this is the Black Plague," said Gary Bauer, Reagan's assistant for domestic policy. "I think only time will tell."

The political response was to establish task forces and committees to study and bury the problem. It was limited to damage control. The government refused to recognize that AIDS was an equal-opportunity disease.

The denial was so complete that in 1986 the National Institutes of Health actually left $47 million appropriated for the testing of AIDS drugs unspent. *Newsday*'s Larry Kramer called the many delays, interdepartmental rivalries, and political fears of the Reagan administration "genocide."

The economic costs of AIDS

Worldwide, the financial drain of AIDS is staggering. By the year 2000, careful estimates suggest, it will drain between $356 billion and $514 billion from the global economy. The latter figure amounts to 1.4 percent of the world's gross domestic product. It is the equivalent of wiping out the economy of Australia or India.

AIDS travels with impunity and without a passport. AIDS will affect hardest the poor countries that can afford it least.

In the U.S., AIDS will siphon off between $81 billion and $107 billion by the year 2000—about 1 percent of the gross domestic product. But in Africa and the Middle East, AIDS-related losses will range from 2.4 to 4.6 percent of the gross domestic product—enough of a loss to wipe out any real economic growth in those regions.

In Thailand, AIDS will kill thousands of people during their most productive years. At the Amsterdam conference, Jonathan Mann, director of Harvard's International AIDS Center, reflected: "Considering what it takes to make one neurosurgeon in a developing country and what it means to lose him is a very clear indication of the societywide impact of AIDS."

Even while they are alive, people who have AIDS produce less and require more, especially in the latter stages of their illness.

At present, proper care for an AIDS patient in the U.S. can amount to $120,000 in direct costs alone. This does not count their own loss of earning power nor that of family members who must take time off from work or school to care for them. It doesn't take into account the number of orphans, estimated at 10 million worldwide, who will be left behind between 1994 and 2000.

The AIDS crisis also has racial and ethnic implications. According to Harlon L. Dalton, writing in *Daedalus*, 36 percent of people with AIDS in the U.S. are African American. In New York City, it is the number one killer of women between the ages of 25 and 34, and 86 percent of these cases are African American or Latino. Furthermore, once blacks get AIDS, they die five times faster than white people with AIDS.

Even while they are alive, people who have AIDS produce less and require more.

Homelessness among AIDS victims may be unraveling the social fabric as much as drugs and crime. Researcher Peter Arno, writing for the Citizens Commission on AIDS in New York and Northern New Jersey, points out that once the Reagan administration cut federal housing subsidies from $30 billion to $8 billion, HIV/AIDS began to show a marked increase among the homeless population.

Typically, cities will provide some level of care for homeless people with AIDS but refuse shelter to HIV-infected people for fear they will pass it on to other homeless people. People with HIV are often driven from jobs and homes by employers and families, adding to the downward spiral.

Deeply ingrained sexism has made women "the missing persons in the AIDS epidemic," according to Kathryn Anastos, writing in *Health/Pac Bulletin*. Physicians badly underdiagnose women—with devastating results. Women pass the disease on to their unborn children. In New York City alone, the Department of Health estimates that between 1,600 and 4,400 newborns are HIV infected.

A troubling health care system

The litany of inequities continues:

- Medicare pays only 1 percent of the total medical bills of people with AIDS. In addition, qualifying periods are usually 24 months, by which time the victim is dead.
- The drug reimbursement program is limited to those not covered by Medicaid and does not cover certain drugs. Medicaid coverage is mined with presumptive barriers.
- Veterans' benefits can help somewhat, but there is always the sticky problem of establishing service- versus nonservice-related illnesses.
- Indigent-care programs, catastrophic health insurance, and high-risk insurance pools are often larded with catch-22s that typically require AIDS sufferers to contribute at least 50 percent of their income or pay the first $10,000.
- Seventy percent of Americans have private insurance. Insurance companies, however, alarmed by the cost of AIDS, are using a variety of methods to avoid providing coverage, claims payments, or both to people with AIDS.
- The need for beds for AIDS patients in New York City is already bankrupting most of the city's hospitals. The strain on New York in the next decade has been described as "unimaginable." Similar problems in other cities will follow.

The moral, ethical, and legal issues are a morass of contradictions. While many churches have a good record of caring for people with AIDS, most still sanction only heterosexual sex within marriage.

Churches are often viewed as homophobic and speak out constantly about what they perceive as a decaying moral order. All that moralizing, however, has failed to halt the disease any more than turn-of-the century hysteria halted syphilis, when World War I soldiers were told that "German bullets are cleaner than a whore."

Some critics hold the Catholic Church's categorical ban on the use of condoms or spermicides responsible for contributing to the spread of AIDS and causing deaths that could have been prevented.

What, then, should happen? Clearly fear of the disease, increased education, compulsory health measures, and development of certain vaccines will not stem the tide. No single avenue will suffice. The only successful approach to the epidemic, according to Dr. Allan M. Brandt, professor at Harvard's Medical School, begins with "a full recognition of the important social, cultural, and biological aspects of AIDS."

Once the priority matches the problem, every world resource must be employed to halt its onset and to find a cure. It will cost billions, almost as much as a war.

It's like Arsenio said. This *is* World War III.

5
Government Efforts to Control the Spread of AIDS Are Ineffective

Tomas J. Philipson, Richard A. Posner, and John H. Wright

Tomas J. Philipson is an assistant professor of economics at the University of Chicago. Richard A. Posner is chief judge of the U.S. Court of Appeals for the Seventh Circuit. John H. Wright is a research fellow at the University of Chicago Law School. Philipson and Posner are the authors of Private Choices and Public Health: The AIDS Epidemic in an Economic Perspective.

Government AIDS prevention programs have been unsuccessful because public health officials have failed to understand the basic difference between the AIDS epidemic and previous epidemics. While other infectious diseases are contracted accidentally via contact with air or water or by eating contaminated food, HIV infection spreads only through the exchange of bodily fluids. Because human exchange of bodily fluids is typically a personal choice, there is a strong "behavioral component" that exists with AIDS. Since humans are rational thinkers who tend to avoid risk, most will alter their behavior to minimize their chances of contracting HIV, thereby controlling the spread of AIDS. Failing to understand this unique nature of the AIDS epidemic, the government continues to increase funding for prevention programs. Unfortunately, studies have indicated that much of the money spent on AIDS programs has been wasted.

Although government's response to the AIDS epidemic may have been tentative at first, its funding of AIDS programs has mushroomed since the mid-1980s. In 1992, the federal and state governments spent $4.9 billion on medical research, HIV testing, education, needle-exchange programs, and other activities. By the end of 1992, total government funding for AIDS had reached nearly $22 billion.

Many people say this is not enough. They cite the gloomy statistics—

Reprinted with permission from *Issues in Science & Technology*, Tomas J. Philipson, Richard A. Posner, and John H. Wright, "Why AIDS Prevention Programs Don't Work," Spring 1994, pp. 33-35.

100,000 new AIDS cases diagnosed and 50,000 more deaths in 1993. But any increased spending on AIDS programs would most likely be misguided. Indeed, a two-year study that we conducted at the University of Chicago indicates that much of the money spent on AIDS has been ineffective in stopping the spread of the epidemic and thus essentially wasted.

Policymakers have devised programs that are as likely to further the spread of AIDS as inhibit it.

AIDS programs have failed, we believe, because government has completely misunderstood the role that human behavior plays in AIDS transmission. As a result, policymakers have devised programs that are as likely to further the spread of AIDS as inhibit it.

In its approach to AIDS, government has relied on epidemiological models successfully used in vanquishing previous epidemics. But the AIDS epidemic is not like past ones, which spread randomly, primarily through air or water. AIDS, because it can be transmitted only via a very limited number of purely biological pathways, has a strong behavioral component. Unfortunately, the conventional epidemiological approach lacks a mechanism to account for individual behavioral changes in response to the presence of a disease, and in particular for the impact of information on behavior. This is important because most government AIDS interventions involve either gathering or disseminating information. Thus, since public programs are based on epidemiological models that cannot account for the effects of information, AIDS program designers and administrators have no way of evaluating the true effects of their programs on the spread of the disease.

The role of economics

The discipline that can provide the necessary mechanisms for properly understanding the spread of AIDS is economics, which, above all else, seeks to explain changes in human behavior, including those motivated by information. Economists recognize that disease risks are seen as costs to most people and that people tend to avoid taking exceptionally large ones. Consequently, economic models can account for the fact that since AIDS is deadly, people will in most cases avoid or at least reduce behaviors that put them at risk of contracting HIV.

Economics predicted that once information about the severity of AIDS and the means of transmission was disseminated, AIDS would become largely self-limiting. That is, the spread of AIDS would slow and then stabilize, held in check by the fact that if it were more dangerous, people would take fewer risks and if it were less dangerous, people would take more chances.

Evidence indicates that people have responded to the risk in just this manner, and that allowing for new definitions of what constitutes AIDS, the number of new cases has stabilized. In San Francisco, for example, once the risks became known, high-risk homosexual men made dramatic changes in their sexual behavior, which in turn has dramatically slowed the spread of the disease within the gay community. Similar changes have occurred among members of another high-risk group, intravenous drug users.

A second study that we conducted—focusing on condom use among young adults between 1984 and 1990—confirms these results. During this period, condom use increased in all regions and among members of all racial groups. The study found that people who live in states with higher AIDS rates were more likely, everything else being equal, to use condoms than those from states with fewer cases. In addition, individuals in urban areas, where AIDS is most concentrated, were more likely to use condoms than those in rural areas.

These findings provide two insights. First, low-risk as well as high-risk individuals will change their behavior. Second, people will change their behavior in rough proportion to the risk that they face—evidence that the spread of AIDS is indeed self-limiting.

Applied logic

In general, the more self-limiting the disease, the weaker the case for government intervention. Consider, for example, subsidized, and in some cases mandatory, HIV testing, which is believed to be a key to limiting the spread of AIDS. For testing to work, though, people must respond to the information that testing provides in such a way that they take fewer risks. Only then would the spread of AIDS slow. It is possible, however, that testing might actually increase the spread of AIDS because a person who tests positive no longer faces the risk of becoming infected and thus has less incentive to behave properly. This could lead to an increase in the level of risky behavior in the population.

The key factor in determining whether risky behavior would increase is the level of information among the people who test negative. In a world of perfect information, those who test negative would know who tests positive and that people who test positive are more inclined to take risks. Thus, uninfected people would be more cautious, offsetting the fewer precautions taken by the people who test positive. The net result is ambiguous, but it is likely that in a world of perfect information risky behavior would decrease.

But we do not live in a world of perfect information. Thus, it is unclear what the actual effect of AIDS testing is. Although it is likely that the two pressures offset each other, the extent to which this happens remains an important but unanswered question.

People will change their behavior in rough proportion to the risk that they face.

One of the largest AIDS prevention expenditures has been for education (more than $700 million in 1990, for example). Although most people assume that education must be helpful, it is not necessarily true that government education programs result in the changes in individual behavior that will slow the spread of AIDS.

The greatest challenge for AIDS educators is to accurately communicate the level of risk, thus enabling people to respond to AIDS in rough proportion to the risk that they face personally. Our research indicates, however, that this is not being done. AIDS education programs consist largely of telling the general population what AIDS is and how it can be transmitted. Indeed, a lot of money has been spent providing incomplete information to people whose risk of infection is actually extremely low, but who, perceiving the risk to be higher than it is, subsequently overprotect themselves. At the same time, too little accurate information is being provided to people whose actual risk is very high, people who, perceiving their risks to be lower than they are, tend to underprotect themselves. In recent years, AIDS has spread to groups that are harder to inform (such as intravenous drug users) and are on average less educated (and therefore less likely to act on information once it is received). Without information that accurately conveys true levels of risk in such a way that it will not be ignored, AIDS will continue to spread within high-risk groups while stabilizing in the general population.

Compounding the problem

An increasingly popular public subsidy is the distribution of free condoms. Our economic analysis, however, indicates that this may not appreciably reduce the spread of the disease. Although condoms make sex safer, they do not provide *complete* protection from contracting HIV. But if people think condoms will do so, they may take more risks and possibly further the disease's spread.

One of the most attractive—and according to studies, most effective—of public programs is the providing of clean hypodermic needles to intravenous drug users. But this too is problematic, because it reduces the risk of AIDS and thus the cost of drug abuse. Such a reduction could lead to more people abusing drugs, which could lead to more risky sexual behavior because people are less likely to take precautions during sex while they are on drugs. Here again, then, there are trade-offs. In addition, such a program may not be necessary since used needles can be disinfected with household bleach, as an increasing number of intravenous drug users understand.

Medical research is one of the largest areas of public funding. Clearly, subsidies for basic research can be defended. The current level of public support, however, may well be too great, since a significant portion of federal spending on AIDS research (about 23 percent of the total 1992 federal spending) involves research into possible cures, vaccines, or ameliorative treatments. Since most of the fruits of such research are commercially appropriable, it could be largely left to the private sector.

Government funding for AIDS programs continues to increase and is widely supported by the public. But as costs rise, questions about the efficiency and effectiveness of specific public policies need to be asked. Consequently, an economic perspective on AIDS policy—with its emphasis on the importance of rational choice and human behavior in shaping the course of the epidemic—can provide a valid and workable framework for the policy debates to come.

6

HIV-Positive Homosexuals Should Be More Sexually Responsible

Michelangelo Signorile

Michelangelo Signorile is the author of Queer In America: Sex, the Media and the Closets of Power *and* Outing Yourself.

Although the AIDS epidemic continues to spread, many gay men continue to have unsafe sex. There appears to be a general lack of responsibility and concern toward prevention in gay populations. Many HIV-positive men who are aware that they carry the virus continue having unsafe sex with uninfected partners. Most AIDS activists and programs emphasize the responsibilities of the uninfected. While the HIV-negative population has a responsibility to protect itself, HIV-positive men also have a responsibility toward the uninfected.

Everywhere you turn these days, it seems, there is another report about the alarming breakdown in safe sex among gay men. In a current study financed by the Centers for Disease Control and Prevention, two-thirds of the gay men participating say they have had unprotected sex in the previous 18 months. And after leveling off in the late 1980's, the H.I.V. infection rate among gay men is once again on the rise.

These reports have not surprised me. In moments of profound carelessness, I have also engaged in unsafe sex. Now I find myself in total uncertainty about my H.I.V. status, yet fearful of being tested.

The chilling statistics, combined with my own predicament, make me question the message most AIDS organizations have been sending in their safer sex education campaigns. In general, they have refused to emphasize the particular responsibilities of H.I.V.-positive men, and they have not been attentive to the needs of H.I.V.-negative men, who often feel guilt-ridden because they are still healthy and are in denial about their vulnerability.

In my own case, it's been three years since I was last tested (negative).

Michelangelo Signorile, "HIV Positive and Careless," *New York Times*, February 26, 1995.

I thought that by now I'd have been tested again. Instead, I'm trying to deal with the war raging inside my head. I'm not sure I want to know the truth, and it's clear that I'm not alone. "As far as I'm concerned, the psychological damage has been far worse than any of the health benefits," says a longtime friend, an AIDS activist who has known for six years that he is H.I.V.-positive. "I'd have been spared six years of knowing."

Unsafe sex

Another reason I'm reluctant to be tested is that I quite honestly don't trust myself when it comes to sexual behavior. Having repeatedly tested negative through the late 80's and early 90's, I began to feel falsely confident—as if I were somehow immune to H.I.V. Those feelings enabled me to have unsafe sex, fueling my desire to be carefree and a risk-taker. Now, feeling uncertain about my H.I.V. status, I've been more responsible and more aware.

Not surprisingly, a Baltimore study from the mid-1980's (backed up by subsequent studies) showed that men who tested negative were more likely to engage in unsafe sex within the first six months after they received their test results, leading researchers to conclude that "disclosure of a negative test may have implied to a study participant that he was in some way 'protected' because previous sexual practices did not lead to H.I.V. infection."

On the other hand, I'm frightened that finding out I was *positive* might also play into my carefree nature, that I might in my darkest moments care little about the concerns of an H.I.V.-negative man.

Several H.I.V.-positive men have confided to me that they regularly engage in unprotected sex.

Several H.I.V.-positive men have confided to me that they regularly engage in unprotected sex, rationalizing that the other guy is responsible for himself and must know what he's doing. "I just tell myself that these guys are probably positive," one said to me, because they didn't demand that he put on a condom. "But I know —and realize later—that I have no way of knowing that."

Greg Scott, an AIDS activist in Washington, believes that he infected some of the "many" men with whom he had unprotected sex long after he found out he was H.I.V.-positive. For several years, during the time that he was at the forefront of AIDS activism, he says he was in denial about his own behavior. "I was resolved to practice safe sex, and my philosophy would not have allowed me to be unsafe," he says. "But using drugs and alcohol allowed me to have sex without condoms. It provided the excuse."

Responsible behavior

These scenarios grip me with fear and sadness. After much thought, I realize that I owe it not only to myself but to my sexual partners to know my H.I.V. status. If I find I am negative, I have a responsibility to keep myself that way, to overcome urges to act in ways that put me at risk—no matter what fuels them and no matter how difficult they may be to fight off. And if I am positive, I have a different but equal responsibility: not to put others at risk, and to understand that not all H.I.V.-negative people are equipped to deal with the responsibilities of safer sex.

That message, about the responsibilities of the H.I.V.-positive, is contrary to what the AIDS establishment—from Gay Men's Health Crisis to Act Up—emphasizes in safer sex education and in political rhetoric.

Many positive men are not taking responsibility for protecting negative men from H.I.V.

"The fact is that they have always placed most if not all of the onus on the H.I.V.-negative person not to become infected," Greg Scott says. "None of us, when we go for testing and counseling, are truly told that we're supposed to be *responsible*—that we, as H.I.V.-positive people, have an enormous, grave responsibility in this." He added, "A lot of the politics of it have been about a fear of stigmatizing positive people. It's an attempt to equalize all people in this fight, but it's a lie, because those of us who are infected have very different responsibilities than those who are not infected."

Ten years ago the gay community was fighting off hate-mongers who were intent on locking up H.I.V.-positive people; as a community we needed to foster self-esteem among H.I.V.-positive gay men and to guard against attempts to stigmatize them. Now it seems that some of what we did for those who are positive was at the expense of those who are desperately trying to remain negative.

"The obvious idea that AIDS prevention is *for* H.I.V.-negative men—those who do not presently have H.I.V.—is a controversial, politically inflammatory assertion" in most AIDS organizations, Walt Odets, a Berkeley clinical psychologist, wrote in the spring 1994 issue of the *AIDS and Public Policy Journal*. He went on: "The confused retort is that AIDS prevention is *for the gay community*. . . . Many H.I.V.-positive men quite understandably have different ideas and feelings about life, and live with different values and objectives than H.I.V.-negative men. Despite what we would like to believe politically, many positive men are not taking responsibility for protecting negative men from H.I.V. and do not see why they should."

As the Republican Congress proposes slashing funds in programs from AIDS prevention campaigns to the National Institutes of Health budget, the gay community has the power to alter the course of the AIDS crisis if we face this challenge and change the things that are in our control. That responsibility now rests with our Byzantine AIDS organizations as well as with each of us as individuals.

7

Society and the HIV-Positive Should Share the Responsibility for AIDS Prevention

Charles A. Erin and John Harris

Charles A. Erin and John Harris wrote the following paper as part of the development of the project for the Commission of the European Communities entitled "AIDS: Ethics, Justice and European Policy." They both work at the Centre for Social Ethics and Policy at the University of Manchester in the United Kingdom.

As the AIDS epidemic grows, so does discrimination toward HIV-positive individuals. Society has an obligation to guarantee that those who are HIV-positive are treated fairly. If society fulfilled this obligation, infected people, as well as those who suspect they might be infected, would likely feel obligated to behave responsibly toward others by having themselves tested and notifying their partners of their HIV status. By fostering an environment that promotes these "reciprocal obligations," the state and society would help control the spread of AIDS.

Like no other crisis humankind has faced, the AIDS pandemic highlights weaknesses in the human psyche. In addition to the physical and mental suffering associated with the virus and syndrome, the person who is HIV seropositive or has AIDS may expect to confront both the rational and the irrational fears of those who are not, or believe that they are not HIV seropositive. These fears are often manifested in suspicion of and hostility towards the former.[1]

It is not difficult to imagine how this phobia may actually contribute to the spread of the disease which is its object. The threat of labelling, stigmatisation or ostracism may deter those who consider themselves to be particularly at risk of infection from disclosing their status, undergo-

Charles A. Erin and John Harris, "AIDS: Ethics, Justice, and Social Policy," *Journal of Applied Philosophy*, vol. 10, no. 2 (1993).

ing voluntary testing, or altering their behaviour in ways which might decrease the likelihood of passing on the virus.[2] Thus does the psychological foment the pathological.

The AIDS pandemic poses unprecedented ethical challenges and calls into question long established principles, in particular those relating to confidentiality in the relationship between the patient and the health care professional and to an individual's right of privacy. Whilst much research has been devoted to the obligations of society generally, and health care professionals specifically, toward the individual who has AIDS, little by comparison has been written on the obligations of those with AIDS themselves, which obligations we believe may be the key to the development of an effective and equitable social policy on AIDS. Underpinning an investigation of these obligations are principles of justice and equality, as well as considerations of personal autonomy and human rights.

It is now clear that the HIV seropositive individual has been discriminated against and denied civil rights. It appears likely that the persisting animosity and prejudice shown the HIV seropositive individual could well be defused by the recognition of a duty of all citizens to disclose HIV status under certain conditions. It is our intuition that we should think in terms of a reciprocity of obligations, that is, in terms of a reciprocity between obligations *of* HIV seropositive individuals and obligations *to* HIV seropositive individuals. Greater recognition of responsibility to others on the part of the HIV seropositive individual, if allied to a concomitant firm commitment to equitable treatment, could perhaps result in greater voluntary testing and, conceivably, in a decrease in the spread of HIV among the non-infected population.

Justice and the principle of equality

However we may like to conceive of justice, many would now recognise that the principle of equality lies at its core.[3] The ethical principle of equality may be stated briefly: each person within a community is entitled to and should be afforded equal respect, concern, and protection. At the basis of this principle is the idea that persons are of equal importance.[4] Justice, construed very loosely as fairness, would lack significance if we did not accept that persons matter equally and hence are equally entitled to fair treatment.

A consequence of the principle of equality is that we should not discriminate unfairly between individual members or groups within a community. In the context of health policy and its reaction to the AIDS pandemic, the principle is vitiated if we do not actively seek to afford all non-infected citizens what protection against infection there exists, or if we do not provide HIV seropositive individuals with adequate care of their symptoms, and therapy, as and when it becomes available, and protection against unfair discrimination.

The role of the state

'The Obligation of Subjects to the Soveraign, is understood to last as long, and no longer, than the power lasteth, by which he is able to protect them', wrote [English philosopher] Thomas Hobbes in *Leviathan*.[5] Thus, for Hobbes, the obligation of citizens to obey the rule of law is predicated upon the State's acceptance of the necessity of protecting citizens from threats to life and liberty.[6] It can be argued that this is the essence of the social contract and the sole justification of the State. We will treat the soveraign's acceptance of the necessity to protect citizens as an obligation recognised by the soveraign although for Hobbes, the soveraign had no obligations to citizens—his thesis was merely that citizens had no obligations to the soveraign in the absence of soveraign protection.

It is now clear that the HIV seropositive individual has been discriminated against and denied civil rights.

Whilst in 1651, when *Leviathan* was first published, the kind of threats to life and liberty against which Hobbes would have 'Soveraigns' protect their 'Subjects' consisted chiefly in those of armed or political aggression from abroad, it appears to be generally true to say that in the 1990s the greatest threats to citizens' lives are borne of inadequate health care provision, famine, and disease at home. Since the early 1980s, AIDS has assumed a position as *potentially* one of the greatest threats to humankind, and, without the promise of a 'miracle cure' in the foreseeable future, the State's duty to protect citizens from this aggressor is among its first and foremost obligations.

Concomitant with the State's obligation to protect citizens' lives, and just as important, are its obligations to afford them equal concern and respect. Those citizens for whom protection against infection with HIV has failed should be shown the same concern and respect as other citizens; they are entitled to the same consideration in access to employment, health care, and other areas of social provision, as any other citizen.

Individual responsibility and the duty to warn

On the other hand, the spread of this virus/syndrome which threatens citizens' lives is not independent of individual citizens' actions. Responsibility for protection against HIV/AIDS cannot be wholly abdicated to the State. The individual has, effectively, the power to protect (as much as it is possible to protect) him-/herself and, if he/she is HIV seropositive, others against infection. Inasmuch as this power lies with the individual, for what, and to what extent, is the individual responsible?

If one is responsible for anything, one is responsible for what one *knowingly* brings about, whether or not this was a hoped for or premeditated result of the action or inaction, and independent of whether that action or inaction was intended.[7] Clearly, this conception of individual responsibility has severe implications for those who are, or have reason for suspecting that they are, HIV seropositive, or who have, or believe that they may have AIDS. If those who know they are or may be HIV seropositive, or know they have or may have AIDS, choose not to share this knowledge with their sexual partners, those with whom they share syringes in drug use, health care professionals, *etc*, that is, if they do not forewarn others of the risks they may be taking on, they will be responsible for subjecting those others to the risk of infection, and thus the risk of death, and responsible for their death if, as a result of their actions, the partners contract, and die of, AIDS. Thus:

> [E]ven though the seropositive individual may be innocent in two senses, (a) have innocently, not recklessly, contracted HIV and (b) be innocent of any intent to infect others, nonetheless they are fully responsible if they knowingly or recklessly expose others to risk.[8]

It is sometimes claimed that all individuals have the obligation to protect themselves and that there is consequently no duty to warn. This principle has two major flaws. The first is that it assumes that people will actually protect themselves in obedience to the principle. The second is that it assumes that the protective steps that they might take will be adequate.

We will just look a little more closely at both these flaws. It may be the case, for example, that all workers at a nuclear plant should wear protective clothing at all times. It does not follow from the soundness of such a rule that worker A, seeing that worker B is without her protective clothing on this particular occasion, has no obligation not to turn on a machine that emits dangerous radiation or to warn worker B before turning on the machinery. Or, even if all *are* wearing protective clothing, that there is no obligation not to increase the dangerous radiation above the levels to which the workers have consented to be exposed and are expecting to receive.

The second flaw is equally important. Since there is no such thing as '*safe* sex', merely less hazardous sex, it is important that each individual makes his or her own informed judgement about the level of risk they are prepared to run in each particular case. One might, for example, think that the risk that one's partner has AIDS is low and that this combined with the further lowering of the risk by practising protected intercourse was an aggregate risk worth running. One's assessment might be different if one knew that the first of the two risks was not small but, rather, 100%. This is why health care professionals often want to know (and rightly) the HIV status of patients for particular procedures even though they take routine precautions against infection during those procedures. Equally, and for the same reasons, patients have a legitimate interest in knowing the HIV status of health care professionals.

Transmission and progression rates

It could be argued that gaps in the state of the art of the epidemiology of AIDS weaken the case for a duty on the individual to disclose his or her HIV or 'at risk' status. In particular, there is currently a less than complete understanding of infectiveness, especially during the interval between seroconversion and the pre-AIDS period. Furthermore, some researchers have questioned the direct relation between infection with HIV and the development of AIDS.[9] However, the vast majority of research into conversion and progression mechanisms and rates seems to indicate very strongly that there exists a high risk of contracting HIV via unprotected sexual intercourse with an infected partner, for example, and that the HIV seropositive individual *will* develop AIDS and, eventually, die as a result.[10] If we are considering the need to protect individuals from HIV we ought, clearly, to accept the worst case scenario.

The typical modes of transmission of HIV involve acts which are at least private, and usually intimate. Thus, it is not unexpected that our thesis regarding the responsibilities of individuals conflicts with social conventions on privacy. Should an individual's supposed right to privacy be protected at all costs? In the context of AIDS where one person's withholding information he or she regards as private puts the life of another at risk, the right to privacy of the former must, we submit, take second place to the latter's right to protection.

However, while, as we have construed it, this right to protection from threats to life is a right both against the State and against the individual, enforcing the right to protection in private relationships between individuals does not appear practicable. Even if the right were enshrined in law, the only feasible way of enforcing it would be by enacting punitive measures against those who neglect their (correspondent) duty to forewarn others of their HIV status and/or compensating those who are the victims of a failure to forewarn. But, from the point of view of the victim, this comes too late.

The alternative we are proposing here might at first blush be interpreted as offering social inducements to the HIV seropositive voluntarily to divulge their status, inducements in the form of guarantees of equitable treatment. That this would be false is a point we will return to shortly.

Privacy and third parties

First, let us consider the involvement of third parties. Our focus here will be on the confidentiality of the patient–health care professional relationship. The question we must try to answer here is whether the health care professional should keep information about a patient's HIV status secret, or, in certain circumstances, be free to disclose it to others. The reasons for confidentiality stem from respect for the patient's autonomy. There is a quasi-contractual aspect involved in that the patient divulges information to the health care professional on the, at least tacit, understanding that the information will go no further. On this basis, patients who might not do so otherwise present for treatment confident in the knowledge that they will not be prejudiced in their public life by what they reveal. Furthermore, if there exists a right to privacy, it can be argued that this should extend to control of personal information and access to it.[11] These are strong grounds for the health care professional's preserving patients' confidences.

However, in the context of AIDS, the right to privacy and the principle of confidentiality can conflict with the moral imperative to *do no harm* (or, if one cannot do no harm, to do the least harm). Preserving the confidence of an HIV seropositive patient where he or she is clearly refusing to notify partners and others at risk can do substantial harm. For example, it may endanger the lives of future sexual partners, or keep previous sexual partners in ignorance of their at-risk status and so endanger their future sexual partners. It may, of course, result in loss of life.

How can we resolve this conflict? One way might be to ask: 'Who has the most to lose?' We do not mean to play down the importance of consent and confidentiality or of respecting the special vulnerability of the HIV seropositive individual, but when persons' very lives are endangered by respecting such principles the protection of those persons must be an overriding concern. Notification of partners (sexual or in drug use) is thus a paramount moral imperative. If all attempts to persuade the HIV seropositive individuals voluntarily to disclose their HIV status to those whom they put at risk fail, the health care professional surely has a moral obligation to disclose in order to prevent lives being put at risk. To fail to do so would make the professional responsible for the fate of those at risk.[12]

Practical implications

Lofty rhetoric is all very well. It would be an easy path to take simply to say that this is the conclusion we reach by performance of an ethical balancing act and to leave the working out of its practical implications to others. But one of the jobs of *applied* philosophy, as we see it, is to take into account the practical difficulties of implementing the recommendations of moral reasoning. A moral principle can have little or no point if its observance is impossible in the real world.

Education What is needed, we believe, is education. We are not talking about the kind of education via the media aimed at scaring people into changing their behaviour patterns—visual images of icebergs and tombstones seem to have had a limited beneficial effect in any case. Firstly, greater awareness of what actually are the modes of HIV transmission is required so that the popular myths surrounding transmission are dispelled and HIV seropositive persons are not treated as pariahs. Furthermore, if, as we suggest, partner notification is an overarching moral imperative, the best way we can see to it that acting on this is maximised is by making citizens aware of the responsibilities of at-risk individuals to their partners, third parties and society generally.

Social Responsibility This is a first step, but it is not enough. In the reality of the modern world it is too much to expect persons to take on these responsibilities when to do so would likely lay them open to unfair discrimination. If the individual's obligation to disclose HIV status is to be taken seriously, the State's obligation to show him/her equal concern and respect must be confirmed and enforced.

Responsibility for protection against HIV/AIDS cannot be wholly abdicated to the State.

These societal obligations can be viewed, and at a practical level should be viewed, not only as a corollary, but as a *sine qua non* of the individual's duty to disclose. Whilst the stance we have taken on the responsibilities of individuals can be interpreted as a strong and independent ground for a duty on the individual to disclose HIV status, there is a sense in which the individual's duty to disclose is also and equally a dimension of the State's obligation to protect citizens from threats to life which is the concomitant of the State's obligation to show all citizens the same concern and respect.

How do these obligations to the HIV seropositive individual translate into real terms? Firstly, we should try our utmost to find a cure, or effective treatments for AIDS. The scientific community has already taken this on and is well supported by the public and private purse, and we will say no more on this. Secondly, we should afford HIV seropositive individuals and those with AIDS protections against unfair discrimination. These active protections should encompass all areas of social provision which bear on their fundamental entitlement to equal concern, respect and protection. HIV seropositive individuals should be treated equitably in the provision of access to health care, employment, education, housing, *etc.* In relation to the duty to disclose HIV status specifically, it must be ensured, we would recommend by legislation, that such disclosure does not jeopardise this equitable treatment.

Insurance There is a particular problem with insurance. Life insurance not only provides security for dependents, but, because of the link with mortgages, also secures many people's access to housing. Something must clearly be done to ensure that the HIV seropositive individual has reasonable access to housing and can provide for his or her dependents. Two policies for ensuring equitable provision of life insurance suggest themselves. How viable these might be will partly turn on the scale of the problem of HIV seropositivity and this will partly turn on the success we have in using measures like these to encourage responsible behaviour and control the spread of the disease. Firstly, we could introduce legislation requiring insurance companies to provide cover for HIV seropositive individuals; the costs could be equalised by loading premiums generally—this is a classic business practice. A second alternative is to utilise national resources. That is, the State would make itself responsible for providing HIV seropositive individuals with mortgages and insurance for their dependents.

The right to privacy and the principle of confidentiality can conflict with the moral imperative to do no harm.

The mechanics of such insurance provision are complicated. It is beyond the scope of this paper to explore in detail how either might work or how the costs would be offset.[13] Clearly a ceiling will need to be set on the HIV seropositive individual's ability to obtain such insurance. It should be sufficient to enable such an individual to enter the housing market at a reasonable level but not so high as to enable that individual to exploit the goodwill of society for the personal enrichment either of himself or his family or friends. We do not believe it to be beyond the wit of man or broker to arrive at some reasonable parameters for these purposes. It must be borne in mind that there will almost certainly be gains in public safety and in diminution of personal risk commensurate with the financial burden of the provision. Indeed our guess is that it will come to seem a small price to pay for doing what's right.

This suggestion would hold good for other fatal conditions if it were part of a comprehensive system of health screening of the type we may expect to be available at some time following the successful mapping of the human genome. Then:

> Premiums should be set as if there was no information available, as if screening were not a feature of existence. If they were set for average life expectancy or illness, or accident expectancy for a particular age, the risk would even out. We must remember that for every terminally ill 20-year-old who might get 'unfair' cover there would

be many whom screening and monitoring would protect from disease or premature death and who would consequently *balance* those who cash in.

Since screening is likely to reduce the vulnerability of the community at large, insurance companies cannot be worse off than they are at present if they are required to set premiums as if no new information existed. For this reason legislation constraining insurance companies might be less controversial than would at first appear.[14]

In effect, what we are recommending here is that the infrangibility of the civil rights of HIV seropositive citizens be confirmed in law. In principle, this may be a truism; in reality, it is a desideratum.

Mandatory testing?

The individual's duty to disclose HIV status seems to presuppose an individual's certain knowledge of his/her HIV/AIDS status. If this was the case, the duty to disclose would appear to require mandatory testing for HIV of all citizens as a prerequisite. Ethically, mandatory testing poses many and complex problems,[15] not the least of which are the challenge to personal autonomy this represents and the consequent violation of the right of all citizens to refuse medical touchings, a right which is legally protected in many jurisdictions; ethics aside, doubts have been voiced about the practicability and economic viability of establishing a system of mandatory testing.[16] However, our thesis does not imply universal mandatory testing as a direct consequence. What we are suggesting is that those who *have reason to suspect* that they may be HIV seropositive or have AIDS, as well as those who *know* that they are HIV seropositive or have AIDS, recognise and shoulder their responsibilities to their partners and relevant third parties. One responsibility of members of the former group is, *a priori*, to be tested for HIV antibody. This testing we believe should remain voluntary, and should be accepted simply because it is the right thing to do, in short because it is ethical. However it is always helpful if doing the right thing coincides with one's interests. This, we believe, would be facilitated by our reciprocity of obligations thesis.

Reciprocity of obligations

To date, it seems there has been no alacrity in the securing of what are, after all, fundamental civil rights for people who are HIV seropositive. The reason for this, we suspect, is that talk of the responsibilities of HIV seropositive individuals and those with AIDS is virtually excluded from the discussion. If the debate is framed in terms of *reciprocal* obligations, the protection of HIV seropositive individuals against discrimination, and the possible desirable consequences which we have been discussing, may be more easily attainable. These conclusions are, at basis, direct implications of a conception of justice.

Our chief concern here has been to identify the fundamental premises on which a social policy may be constructed which will help create an environment in which HIV seropositive individuals will not be subject to discrimination and fear of discrimination will not deter the individuals who know or have reason to suspect that they are HIV seropositive or have AIDS from forewarning their partners, or other third parties who they consider may be at risk, of their HIV status.

Notes

1. E.g. Blendon, E.G. & Donelan K. (1988) Discriminating against people with AIDS, *New England Journal of Medicine* 319 pp. 1022–1026.
2. Ferdinand Schoeman makes just this point (Schoeman, F. (1991) AIDS and privacy, in: F.G. Reamer (Ed.) *AIDS & Ethics* pp. 240–276, (New York, Columbia University Press) pp. 241–242):

   > Tragically, fear of discrimination is itself an important obstacle to both greater epidemiological understanding of HIV transmission and implementation of public health measures aimed at minimizing HIV infection.

3. For example, in deriving his conception of justice as fairness, John Rawls' starting point is the 'original position of equality' (Rawls, J. (1971) *A Theory Of Justice* (Oxford, Oxford University Press) pp. 11ff.). See also Dworkin's discussion (Dworkin, R. (1977) *Taking Rights Seriously* (London: Duckworth) Chapter 6).
4. Consider, for example, Robert Nozick's conception (Nozick, R. (1974) *Anarchy, State, And Utopia* (Oxford, Basil Blackwell) p. 33):

   > [N]o moral balancing act can take place among us; there is no moral outweighing of one of our lives by others so as to lead to a greater overall *social* good.

   Also, for Ronald Dworkin (Dworkin, *op. cit.*, p. 199):

   > [T]he weaker members of a political community are entitled to the same consideration and respect of their government as the more powerful members have secured for themselves.

5. Hobbes, T. (1991) *Leviathan* (Cambridge: Cambridge University Press) Chapter 21, p. 153.
6. We are grateful to Stephen Clark for helping to clarify Hobbes's point.
7. Harris, J. (1980) *Violence And Responsibility* (London, Routledge & Kegan Paul) *passim.*
8. Harris, J. (1991) AIDS; ethics and justice, a paper presented at *Colloquio Internazionale: AIDS, Giustizia e Politica Sanitaria,* Milan.
9. Duesberg, P.H. (1991) AIDS epidemiology: inconsistencies with human immunodeficiency virus and with infectious disease, *Proceedings of the National Academy of Science, USA,* 88, pp. 1575–1579.
10. E.g., Hessol, N. A., *et al* (1988) The natural history of HIV infection in a cohort of homosexual and bisexual men—a decade of follow-up, presented at the *Fourth International Conference On AIDS,* Stockholm; Buchbinder, Susan, *et al* (1991) HIV disease progression and the impact of prophylactic therapies in the San Francisco City Clinic cohort—a 13 year follow-up, presented at the *Seventh International Conference On AIDS,* Florence.
11. For a more detailed discussion of confidentiality in the patient–health care professional relationship see, for example, Harris, J. (1985) *The Value Of Life* (London: Routledge & Kegan Paul) pp. 25ff.
12. We are assuming the moral symmetry of acts and omissions—see Harris

(1980) *op. cit.* For an alternative discussion (of how this distorts the patient–health care professional relationship), see Anon., 'Medical confidentiality', *Briefings in Medical Ethics* 7 (1990) 2–3.

13. For a detailed discussion of insurance in the context of health monitoring and screening, see Harris, J. (1992) *Wonderwoman And Superman: The Ethics Of Human Biotechnology* (Oxford: Oxford University Press) Chapter 11.
14. Harris, (1992), *op. cit.*, p. 223.
15. E.g., Childress, J. F. (1991) Mandatory HIV screening and testing in: F.G. Reamer (Ed.) *AIDS & Ethics*, pp. 50–76 (New York, Columbia University Press).
16. Orr, A. (1990) The legal implications of AIDS and HIV infection in Britain and the United States in: Brenda Almond (Ed.) *AIDS—A Moral Issue: The Ethical, Legal And Social Aspects*, pp. 112–139 (Basingstoke: The MacMillan Press).

8

Routine Testing Is Needed to Control the Spread of AIDS

Helen Mathews Smith

Helen Mathews Smith is the former editor of MD *magazine. She is now writing a book on the HIV/AIDS epidemic.*

Education, needle-exchange programs, and "safe-sex" campaigns have all failed to control the spread of AIDS. The Public Health System's response to the AIDS epidemic has been missing a key component of basic plague control strategy: mandatory testing and tracking. By requiring everyone to test regularly for HIV infection and notifying all sexual partners of those individuals who test positive for HIV, the AIDS epidemic could be controlled and even eliminated. Many, including the American Civil Liberties Union and gay rights groups, argue that required testing and partner notification would violate individuals' right to privacy. Unfortunately, public health officials have conceded to pressure exerted by these groups. While public health control policy continues to focus on those who are not infected, the HIV-positive who are ignorant of their condition unknowingly continue to spread the disease. The need to control the AIDS epidemic and save lives must take precedence over individuals' right to privacy.

Education has not worked; neither have clean needles nor lectures on "safe sex." We have condomized America, but the AIDS epidemic still rages out of control—not because of ignorance, but because narrow political interests have undermined the standards and traditions of the officials responsible for the nation's health.

For more than a decade, American public health officials have pursued a failed strategy. They have ignored the central tenets of plague control: routine testing, tracking the path of the disease, and warnings to those at risk. Because HIV infection has been given a unique legal and medical status, says Denver's director of public health, Dr. Franklyn N.

Helen Mathews Smith, "Are We Nuts?" Reprinted with permission from the Autumn 1995 issue of the *Women's Quarterly*, published by the Independent Women's Forum.

Judson, "we have gotten off track" with a national strategy that is "irrational, erroneous, and unethical."

Inappropriate public health policy

From the very beginning of the crisis, public health officials have seemed incapable of an appropriate response. Even though it was clear by the early 1980s that gay bathhouses were a deadly breeding ground for AIDS, Dr. Mervyn Silverman, the director of the San Francisco Department of Public Health, took three years to decide whether to regulate or close down the bathhouses. In an interview with Frances FitzGerald for her book *Cities On A Hill*, Silverman said: "I may look as if I'm responding to political pressures, but what I'm responding to is opposition from the gay community. . . . If gays start opposing my decisions—if they start looking on me as a heavy father—then the whole issue of AIDS gets lost."

And the last thing any public health official wants to do is play the "heavy." In the early 1980s, Dr. David Axelrod, then-commissioner of health for New York State, described efforts to close bathhouses as "ridiculous." He also refused to classify AIDS as a sexually transmitted disease. As a result, and with the support of Governor Mario Cuomo, the testing and partner-notification regulations that apply to syphilis and gonorrhea do not apply to HIV infection in New York State.

Things haven't gotten much better in the intervening decade. When a new wave of sex clubs opened in New York City in 1993, city health commissioner Margaret A. Hamburg suggested that working with the clubs might be more helpful than shutting them down. "Our goal," said Hamburg, "is to reduce high risk behavior through education."

This was certainly not the style of London's Dr. John Snow. In 1854, when Snow traced an outbreak of cholera to the Broad Street pump, he didn't hold a consensus conference or ask local shopkeepers for permission to shut it down. The pump had to go, said Snow, because it was killing people, and city officials removed it. Snow, by the way, didn't know what caused cholera, and he certainly didn't have a cure for it—but he saved a great many lives. There are few public officials like Snow anymore.

The spread continues

The collapse of the nation's AIDS strategy is undebatable. The federal government has spent tens of millions of dollars on education, group counseling, and behavior-modification research. It has spawned a huge bureaucracy of AIDS social workers and neighborhood activists whose livelihood depends on what government publications describe as "culturally sensitive, community-based programs."

Two out of three middle and upper schools in the nation offer AIDS education courses, and the Centers for Disease Control and Prevention (CDC), the federal agency responsible for the public's health, publishes hundreds of pamphlets and brochures. The Gay Men's Health Crisis (GMHC), the largest AIDS activist group in the nation, with a budget of about $18 million a year, also has educational programs. None of these efforts has been able to stem a second tide of infection. Increased rates began showing up in the late 1980s, but it was not until 1995 that any media attention was given to the annual 2.5 percent increase in HIV infection among young gay men.

Since 1981, almost half-a-million cases of AIDS have been reported, and every year there are forty thousand new infections. Over sixty thousand women have been diagnosed with AIDS, and about half of the cases were reported between 1991 and 1995. The sharpest rate of increase is not among drug addicts, but among young black and Hispanic women infected through heterosexual sex.

In 1994, for the first time in the history of the epidemic, the ratio of young women to men shifted: more adolescent girls were infected than boys, and almost three-fourths did not know their partners were HIV-positive. Add high rates of youth alcoholism and drug abuse, and you have the next leading edge of the virus among all races.

Civil rights vs. saving lives

What happened? Gay activist and writer Michelangelo Signoreli gave one explanation in an essay in the *New York Times* in February 1995. Signoreli made the point that out of a fear of "stigmatizing" AIDS-infected people, AIDS organizations have "placed most if not all of the onus on the HIV-negative person not to become infected." It is precisely this bias that is one of the root causes of the government's failure to contain the epidemic.

Widespread HIV testing was discouraged by public health officials to protect the civil rights of the infected, but unless those who are infected know their HIV status, they can neither protect their sexual partners nor get early treatment for themselves. After heated debate, and years of opposition from the ACLU and AIDS activists, New York State finally passed a law in 1995 permitting a rape victim to request an HIV test from the man convicted of raping her. Until then, a victim did not have the right to know whether her rapist was also her executioner. Testing continues to be characterized by public health officials as an individual choice—never an obligation. In spite of a horrifying infection rate of twelve percent for men and twenty percent for women in New York State prisons, HIV tests are still not required even of inmates.

Mandatory testing of newborns

I met two of the victims of America's failed war on AIDS at the Incarnation Children's Center in New York City, an eighteen-bed AIDS hospice and clinic in Harlem. Isabel Argueta is a small woman with short dark hair, olive skin, and an oval face. Beside her was her three-year-old son, Jonathan—a frail looking boy wearing chocolate-colored shorts that came down almost to his ankles.

When Jonathan was eight months old, he became deathly ill with pneumocystis carinii pneumonia (PCP), and it was only then that Argueta discovered that they were both HIV-positive. When she told Jonathan's father, he packed his bags, moved in with another woman, and then left for Central America where he is now dying of AIDS. Argueta says Jonathan's father was bisexual and involved with drugs, but she doesn't think he was ever tested for HIV. If he was, he never told her about it. She insists that neither before nor during her pregnancy was she asked to take an HIV test. Like the vast majority of infected women in America, Argueta did not find out she was sick until someone in her family became ill.

Jonathan, however, was not totally lost to government epidemiologists. On his birthday—July 29,1992—he became a case number in an anonymous forty-four-state study to track the epidemic, organized and financed by the CDC. The founding director of the Incarnation Children's Center, Dr. Stephen W. Nicholas—a professor of pediatrics at the College of Physicians and Surgeons of Columbia University who helped care for Jonathan—shakes his head in dismay. "Anonymous testing by the CDC," says Nicholas, "showed that since 1988 we had a major problem; we were not diagnosing AIDS until the child got sick."

If they are diagnosed at birth, adds Nicholas, "HIV babies can have longer, higher-quality lives. For over a decade, I have witnessed grief-stricken mothers and fathers learn of their own HIV infections as their baby lay dying in their arms from a preventable pneumonia. Those opposed to testing pregnant women and infants say the stress of knowing the truth is too much for them. Is there less stress in seeing your three-month-old child die? How much more stress would you like?"

HIV infection has been given a unique legal and medical status.

In New York State, AIDS activists opposed testing for other reasons, adds Nicholas, "and as a result many women were discouraged from finding out if they were infected. The counseling message was, 'Get a test, but it may wreck your life.' Counseling and education failed. What we needed to get a handle on the epidemic was an effective public health system—we didn't have it."

The director of research at the Pediatric AIDS Foundation in Novato, California, Dr. Arthur J. Ammann, says the problem is nationwide. "Once treatment for HIV-infected babies was available in the late 1980s, anonymous testing by the CDC should have been abandoned immediately, and all those infected identified." And when it was discovered in 1994 that the drug AZT could prevent the transmission of AIDS from an infected mother to her newborn there was, says Ammann, another reason "to change the rules." No infant, he adds, "would refuse a treatment capable of turning the risk of dying from a prolonged and painful disease into one of a normal life, but that is precisely the problem: Infants cannot be asked."

Ammann has compared the CDC's anonymous testing of infants to the notorious Tuskegee study that followed four hundred black Alabama sharecroppers infected with syphilis to study the disease's progression. Begun in the early 1930s, the Tuskegee "experiment," financed by the Public Health Service, should have been abandoned when penicillin became available in the 1940s. It was not—for more than a quarter-century—until someone stumbled across these unfortunate men in 1972. Ironically, it was the moral outrage of liberal academics that made the Tuskegee study famous. A research subject's right to informed consent was sacred, but the same groups that defended exploited sharecroppers are silent on the subject of AIDS research upon infants. The drugs are different, but the moral issue is the same.

How did the public health system fail? An early preview of the coming crisis occurred at the Atlanta meeting held by the CDC in February 1987 to examine the future role of HIV testing. The agency's director, Dr. James Mason, said the meeting "was called to apply the best science, the best logic and wisdom to the task of controlling this unprecedented epidemic." The two-day conference—a cross between a university teach-in and a political convention—was attended by eight hundred people, including state and federal health officials, and the representatives of nineteen organizations, from the ACLU, the GMHC, and the National Gay and Lesbian Task Force, to the American Association of Physicians for Human Rights.

To track the path of the epidemic, the CDC proposed testing new groups, including pregnant women, marriage license applicants, and hospital patients. AIDS activists strongly opposed the new strategy. They argued that wider testing was unnecessary, expensive, and raised civil rights issues that would have to be resolved. They advocated instead more counseling and a mass-education campaign targeted to the general public. For teenagers, they recommended candid discussions of sex and condoms; for drug addicts, needle exchange programs. At the time, William Bennett, then-secretary of education, thought it was the wrong approach. Under certain circumstances, he said, mandatory testing might be needed, and kids may also need to hear about the "virtue of restraint." Bennett's remarks made a few headlines, but in Atlanta—where the important public health decisions were being made—no one was listening.

In the end, the medical establishment voted for individual rights. The prestigious Institute of Medicine, a committee of the National Academy of Sciences, declared that, "mandatory screening of at-risk individuals is not an ethically acceptable means for attempting to reduce the transmission of infection." But it was then-Surgeon General C. Everett Koop who settled the matter. From the nation's public health bully pulpit, Dr. Koop wrote: "Compulsory blood testing of individuals is not necessary. The procedure could be unmanageable and cost-prohibitive."

"The need for legislation to protect the rights of AIDS victims was endorsed by everyone present," wrote a *New York Times* reporter, "from dark-suited federal officials to jeans-clad advocates of homosexual rights."

The collapse of the nation's AIDS strategy is undebatable.

An unexpected conclusion that was also a radical departure from public health principles. Exactly fifty years earlier, in 1937, President Franklin D. Roosevelt's surgeon general began a campaign against syphilis that advocated the opposite strategy. Faced by an appalling toll of death and deformity among infants with syphilis, Surgeon General Thomas Parran accused "public health officials and physicians of passivity in the face of misery." He organized an aggressive testing and partner notification system—before the discovery of penicillin—that brought the infant and adult epidemic under control.

Yet while Koop caved in to the activists, U.S. blood banks began testing for HIV infection in March 1985, and soon after the Department of

Defense began testing all active duty personnel and new recruits. The procedures were neither unmanageable nor cost-prohibitive. The military did the test for three dollars, and blood banks dramatically reduced the number of transfusion-related infections. By the end of 1986, eight state health departments had begun successful programs of routine HIV testing and mandatory reporting. Two states that began HIV testing in 1986—Colorado and Minnesota—were and are today state models of disease control, common sense, and compassion.

Common sense, however, was no match for the rhetorical skills of the AIDS activists. The activists insisted that mandatory testing was a slippery slope toward detention camps. A few months after the conference in May 1987 the CDC offered two minor concessions to the traditions of epidemiology: It recommended that high-risk groups be "encouraged" to take the HIV test, but warned that individuals should not be tested unless they had received "appropriate counseling" and had given their consent. People have "a right to choose not to be tested" for HIV, said the CDC, and counseling should be "non-judgmental." Mandatory testing should be discouraged, continued the agency, because it was not the best use of money or personnel. As for pregnant women, those at risk were "encouraged" to take the test.

Difficulty tracking the epidemic

Voluntary testing, however, created major problems for the CDC. Without routine testing to track the epidemic, the agency was faced with the consequences of planned ignorance. Because HIV infection can take as long as a decade to mature into full-blown AIDS, the number of AIDS cases told the agency where the epidemic had been ten years ago—not where it was going. To fill the data hole, the CDC financed studies at methadone and venereal disease clinics, as well as the forty-four-state survey of newborns that had included baby Jonathan. The HIV test was added to a routine infant test for genetic and infectious diseases, including sickle-cell anemia and syphilis.

AIDS activists did not object to this survey because, since it was anonymous, the results could not be traced to the mother. What they couldn't know was that six years later, the survey would provoke a major political crisis in Albany and Washington. Nettie Mayersohn, a Democratic Assemblywoman from Queens, embarked on a personal crusade to get HIV-infected infants identified and treated. In 1993, she proposed a bill in the New York State Assembly that would unblind the CDC study and make notification of the infant's mother mandatory. Leaning half across her desk, Mayersohn says angrily: "I simply couldn't believe it. In New York State, a baby had become a number."

Mayersohn's bill has been blocked by the Democratic leadership of the assembly. AIDS activists and feminist groups are vehemently opposed to it, and the bill has sharply divided the medical community. The ACLU insists that the bill would violate New York State's tough HIV law, which requires written consent for an HIV test. The ACLU may be right: The 1988 law, pushed through the assembly without any debate, has been a major stumbling block to wider HIV testing.

In March 1995, a Newborn HIV Notification Act modeled after the

Mayersohn bill was introduced in the House of Representatives. It brought a quick response from the Clinton administration. Nat Hentoff reported in the *Village Voice* that Congressman Gary Ackerman, a Democrat from Queens who sponsored the bill, had a visit from Dr. David Satcher, the head of the CDC, and Patricia Fleming, the White House's coordinator of AIDS policy. Satcher told Ackerman "that if he insisted on going ahead with this bill to unblind the infant test, the CDC would withdraw the study," Hentoff wrote. Ackerman refused, and in May the CDC, under orders from the White House, suspended the test.

Widespread HIV testing was discouraged by public health officials to protect the civil rights of the infected.

In July, the CDC published its recommendations for the testing of pregnant women—returning to a position it briefly held in the winter of 1986. "Because of advances, particularly in the use of AZT to prevent newborn AIDS," the CDC guidelines recommended "routine HIV counseling and voluntary testing for all pregnant women." The phrase "voluntary testing" makes it dear that the agency is still stuck in the murky politics of the 1987 Atlanta meeting.

Some progress has been made, though: Instead of testing just high-risk women, the CDC now recommends that "all" pregnant women should be tested. [And on October 10, 1995, as part of a legal settlement, New York Governor George Pataki announced that he would unblind the New York infant AIDS test and make the results available to their mothers.] But the CDC still refuses to pose—let alone answer—the fundamental question: Can the nation continue to depend upon voluntary testing to bring this deadly epidemic under control?

A need for change

In 1987, women represented four percent of AIDS cases; today they are almost twenty percent. In 1994, eight thousand infants were born to HIV-infected mothers. Of the 1.3 million HIV-infected Americans, fewer than half have been tested. The situation is so grave that the FDA is considering approval of an HIV home test kit, promoted by—of all people—Dr. C. Everett Koop, who says the nation has failed to pursue all options in identifying those infected.

Does the country really need the privatization of AIDS testing? And who would track the sexual contacts of those who test themselves at home, when twenty-five state health departments—including those of the states with the highest rates of infection, Florida, California, Texas, and New York—do not report HIV cases by name?

When I spoke to him in Atlanta in 1988, Michael T. Osterholm, the director of epidemiology of the Minnesota Department of Health, said, "The time to deal with the crisis is now. In five years it will be too late. Perceived risk—not education—changes behavior, and that is the greatest value of HIV testing."

Osterholm was right. Denver's public health director, Franklyn Judson, explains why: "The CDC continues to reflect the pressures they are under. They strive for consensus—and what you get are contradictory, unclear guidelines." In Denver, says Judson, "the HIV test has been routinely offered to everyone at risk since the mid-1980s. We have had five thousand cases of AIDS, and three thousand deaths, but no one has lost their confidentiality because of the public health department."

The basic goals of HIV testing are surveillance and reporting, adds Judson, but we also have a duty to warn the uninfected and to break the chain of transmission that keeps the epidemic alive. Judson warned in 1989 that "voluntarism will not work for some individuals, and society must choose between effective public health law—including restrictive measures—now, or a much larger reservoir of HIV infection and more deaths from AIDS for many generations to come."

Dr. Sanford F. Kuvin, the vice chairman of the National Foundation for Infectious Diseases, says, "We have been betting on the wrong horse for fourteen years. One hundred thousand women of child-bearing age are infected, and clearly CDC voluntarism has failed. All pregnant women should be mandatorily tested for HIV, have mandatory counseling, and—if positive—be offered AZT during pregnancy."

Would mandatory or routine testing bring an end to the epidemic? No one can know. But at the very least, lives would be saved, and public health policy would no longer represent a retreat from common decency and sense. The nation has a moral duty to care for those who are infected, but the infected also have a responsibility to those with whom they share their lives—and bodies. Public health officials once enforced that responsibility. They need to do so again.

9

Mandatory Testing of Infants Will Not Control the Spread of AIDS

Lisa Merkel-Holguin

Lisa Merkel-Holguin is the Child Welfare League of America's program manager for HIV/AIDS.

Some AIDS officials believe that newborns should be tested for HIV at birth, and that their parents or guardians should be notified of the results so that appropriate action can be taken to save infected children. Although this may appear to be an appropriate strategy to combat the growing problem of HIV-infected babies, a closer examination reveals flaws. Testing an infant for HIV at birth is inaccurate, and infants who are determined to be HIV-positive will not automatically receive treatment. Furthermore, a mandated testing program that lacks a complementary and accessible treatment program will likely scare away mothers who learn unexpectedly of their HIV-positive status. A better strategy would be to promote voluntary testing before, during, and after pregnancy and provide counseling and support to expectant HIV-positive mothers. A mother's approval and cooperation are needed in order to help her and her baby. When surrounded by an atmosphere of mutual trust and respect, most mothers agree to testing and treatment.

Legislation has been introduced in several states and in the U.S. House of Representatives that would undo the confidentiality of the epidemiological surveillance data on the HIV status of newborns now collected anonymously in 44 states by the Centers for Disease Control and Prevention (CDC). Under the proposed federal legislation, the Newborn Infant HIV Notification Act, the parent, legal guardian, or state official responsible for each newborn would be notified of the child's HIV status.

At first glance this seems like a modest proposal. A number of prominent individuals and organizations have expressed their support for it without much more than a first glance. On close examination, however, it has serious drawbacks for infants, mothers, and society at large. CWLA [Child Welfare League of America] is opposed to both mandatory disclosure of infant test results and mandatory HIV testing. The facts are these:

• Infant testing doesn't test infants; it tests mothers. All children of HIV-positive mothers test positive at birth, but less than 25% of them are still positive after 18 months. Revealing the HIV status of these infants, whose mothers never agreed to testing or disclosure, would violate the mother's right to informed consent.

• None of the current proposals would do anything to reduce HIV transmission from mother to child. According to a study released in the fall of 1994 (ACTG 076), the drug AZT can reduce the risk of perinatal HIV transmission by 67% if it is administered to the mother in the second trimester and during birth, then to the infant during the first six weeks of life. Treating only the child after birth does not produce such results.

• The proposals wouldn't reduce transmission through breastfeeding either, because mothers who choose breastfeeding will have been nursing for three weeks before they receive the CDC test results.

Testing at birth is too late to serve any purpose other than that of epidemiological surveillance.

• A mother who learns, with no preparation, that she is HIV positive and her baby is at risk may be driven away from the health care system. No one can help her or the baby without her consent and cooperation. Most mothers agree to testing and treatment when they are offered in the context of a relationship where trust has been established and help is forthcoming.

• The proposed federal legislation mandates counseling, but provides no funds for either counseling or treatment. A mandate to test does not necessarily lead to treatment. The incidence of sexually transmitted diseases is still on the rise in New York State, despite mandatory testing of pregnant women.

• Comparisons to other diseases for which results are currently revealed ignore important differences: first, the stigma attached to HIV/AIDS, and second, the fact that there is no cure.

• Some proponents would treat all HIV-positive infants for Pneumocystis Carinii Pneumonia (PCP), a complication of HIV, but doctors do not know what risk this might involve for the 75% of HIV-positive infants who are not actually infected.

Many organizations that opposed New York's original legislation supported a later bill that called for mandatory counseling and voluntary testing. Clearly, however, our best hope is in providing a comprehensive array of culturally competent health care and social services, including prevention activities, counseling, and voluntary HIV testing, to all women before, during, and after pregnancy. Encouraging women to be tested for HIV early in pregnancy can help health providers plan for effective prenatal care, including admission into clinical trials. Testing at birth is too late to serve any purpose other than that of epidemiological surveillance—the purpose that CDC's testing program was designed to accomplish.

10

AIDS Prevention Programs Should Utilize Traditional Disease Control Methods

William B. Kaliher

William B. Kaliher has worked for many years in the field of disease control and is currently chairman of the Disease Control Section of the South Carolina Public Health Association.

Accurate testing and contact tracing should be the basic components of any successful sexually transmitted disease program. Unfortunately, AIDS prevention officials continue to avoid the utilization of such traditional techniques, bowing to the pressures of gay rights groups determined to protect the identity of AIDS victims. As a result, America's national AIDS program is ineffective and many lives are being unnecessarily sacrificed.

Try this one! The Fairy Godmother suddenly picked you to manage a national trucking concern. She had giant warehouses and trucking facilities in every state, good drivers for every truck, top radio operators for every terminal, an excellent sales staff, a proven administrative staff to ensure that cargoes are picked up appropriately, bills paid and collected, and taxes filed. She gave you a fine management team and told you to develop the trucking operation within six months.

Even with no background in management or trucking, you would study existing trucking operations and use your trained personnel to establish routes, obtain business and do what is necessary to compete, and be successful as a trucking company.

Now, instead of a trucking company, make the company a federal organization assigned to fight AIDS. You would think that doctors, nurses, social workers, and investigators would be assigned to perform the correct duties and do the jobs for which they had been trained and had experience. You would assume that the program would be based on a proven, successful system already in operation.

William B. Kaliher, "Is There a National AIDS Program?" *Conservative Review*, September/October 1995. Reprinted by permission.

Unfortunately for the taxpaying public, quite the opposite occurred with the AIDS program. Existing disease control programs were ignored. Established routes and procedures were immediately destroyed. Nurses, social workers and others with no interview experience were assigned investigative work. Health educators were often used to manage the disease control aspect of the program. Had this been the trucking operation, the AIDS program managers would have assigned the secretaries and clerks to drive the trucks, and conversely the drivers would have taken over management and bookkeeping.

Bizarre, crazy, insane, but that is exactly what occurred with the federal money that should have built an AIDS control program. The United States had an established Sexually Transmitted Diseases (STDs) and TB program but the managers of the AIDS programs chose not to utilize what was tried and true. Instead, they seemed to pick individuals who were least likely to be successful in achieving their goals. Individual health care workers wanted to do a good job, but it seems AIDS management asked who or what profession will ensure a poor over-all job and bingo! There was the hundred-pound secretary suddenly behind the 18-wheeler, and the great driver with a tenth-grade education acting as bookkeeper. The first training session for AIDS counseling and contact elicitation in one of the few states to have that much of a program was attended by five "Aunt Bee" types from "Mayberry," because it was claimed that Venereal Disease Investigators were too harsh to deal with homosexual problems. It didn't matter that the investigators had been working with secretive homosexuals for years. Now they were too harsh and instead "older ladies" were going to counsel AIDS patients and learn about different types of gay sex, from eating feces to gerbiling.

Fifteen years after recognition of the first AIDS patients, it is difficult to believe the decisions to fail were accidental. A sane person with no medical background would have waited a few weeks, asked people what the different roles were in different jobs and come up with an AIDS program that had a definite disease control component, just as a person off the street would have operated a trucking concern properly.

Where the [Sexually Transmitted Disease] programs have established management principles and definite goals, you learn that there is no commonality in the AIDS programs among states.

Interviews with health care workers from South Carolina, New York, Georgia, Florida, Michigan, Arkansas, Texas, Alabama, and Mississippi consistently reveal that no AIDS program has the accountability mechanisms, the data or statistical collection ability, the cohesiveness, or concern over production that is found in the Sexually Transmitted Disease programs. All aspects of good interviewing and investigative techniques are lacking. Where the STD programs have established management principles and definite goals, you learn that there is no commonality in the AIDS programs among states.

A preacher is named as a contact by five individuals infected with syphilis. The preacher is contacted but tells the health care worker he refuses testing and/or treatment. The worker explains the law (found in most states) requiring named contacts or people potentially carrying a communicable disease to be examined and treated if necessary. The preacher is examined and treated because he knows a warrant will be signed if he does not deal with the communicable disease properly. Then the preacher is no longer able to spread the infection.

But the fact is, there is such a preacher, who has been named by five different people with the AIDS virus, and not only has he refused testing but he is continuing an active sex life.

The truth is that the most basic aspects of any disease control program, accurate testing and reporting, contact follow up, etc., *are either not done or are done in a haphazard manner.*

There are general federal and state AIDS programs, but if the funding that is strictly for medical research is separated, and the disease control aspects of AIDS programs are examined, one must conclude there is either no program or the program is designed to increase AIDS.

The public assumes there is a program designed to halt the spread of AIDS. The public, and even much of the medical community, thinks there is a disease control aspect to AIDS on the level of the STD and TB programs, and that patients are being properly followed by the state. Yet the truth is that the most basic aspects of any disease control program, accurate testing and reporting, contact follow up, *etc.*, are either not done or are done in a haphazard manner.

Hypothetical or real

The horror involved with the example of the preacher is not the least of the problems found in the so-called AIDS programs. Suppose that a man traveling through a state having some semblance of an AIDS program tests positive, but returns to his home state before his positive test results are reported. The man's name, address and other pertinent information are phoned to the AIDS program in his state so he can be notified and followed. The man's home state refuses to take any information on his location, and only wants his age and race for some obscure statistical purpose. The man is able to return to his wife, quite unaware that he has a disease he may spread to her.

Imagine that you have traveled to South Carolina in the past year and had sex with someone. A month later that individual is diagnosed with syphilis and is interviewed. Your name is obtained and someone in your state gives you notice that you need to have testing and treatment. But now imagine that your sexual contact is diagnosed with AIDS. Your partner might or might not be interviewed for AIDS, but even if he or she is interviewed, it is unlikely that you are lucky enough to be living in a state that has an AIDS program that will ensure you are notified of your risk.

These are not hypothetical examples. Such incidents have been repeated hundreds if not thousands of times.

This is our national AIDS program and effort, an unmitigated failure, a program so poor at utilizing tax dollars it makes the Pentagon buying hammers at five hundred dollars apiece seem like a bargain in comparison. The reasons are numerous, but too many of those reasons come back to homosexuality. It appears that the gay leadership, not the average homosexual, has fought against using the basic tenets of disease control to stop this disease. Groups such as ACT-UP and Queer Nation have constantly fought against contact tracing and reporting test results by name, and these are the two most basic elements needed to control a sexually transmitted disease.

The fact is that the STD program has functioned for years based on confidentiality. It has never identified gay individuals or caused them to be ousted from their communities, despite interviewing, testing and following their contacts for the diseases of syphilis and gonorrhea.

We have the problem of a press often totally in favor of what certain homosexuals declare to be homosexual rights. The media might look into the fraud, mismanagement and boondoggle that is the AIDS program, except for fear of being targeted as homophobes no matter how accurate their reporting.

It must be asked whether so-called closet queens or married bisexuals have had far too much influence on the AIDS program. Have such individuals, while receiving state or federal money for salaries, been working to push the agenda of certain gay groups instead of the wishes of the majority of the population to control the spread of AIDS? Often these managers are supported by wealthy and powerful gay individuals who fear a real AIDS program and put their fear of public exposure before the good of keeping the infection from spreading to more people.

It appears that the gay leadership, not the average homosexual, has fought against using the basic tenets of disease control to stop this disease.

People managing AIDS programs should have to declare their sexuality and be tested on a regular basis. The unchecked spread of this disease to young people is too important to allow unscrupulous managers to purposely make a disease control program fail, or for good reporters to shy from stories lest they be branded homophobic.

One solution is to defund the AIDS program that now exists and then rehire those people under a program like the STD or TB program. The current personnel would be utilized more properly and have a greater impact working within a program that is consistent across the nation and whose primary goal is to halt the spread of disease.

This would be a godsend to those who really want to control AIDS.

11

AIDS Prevention Programs Should Target Women

Deborah Johnson

Deborah Johnson is working on a book on children and AIDS. Her research has been partially funded by the Center for Economic Policy Research on Women and Gender at Stanford University and the Henry J. Kaiser Family Foundation in support of the Stanford Health Promotion Resource Center.

Heterosexual transmission of the virus that causes AIDS continues to rise. Women face a much greater risk than men of becoming infected with HIV during heterosexual intercourse. Nevertheless, the large majority of AIDS prevention campaigns and public service announcements (PSAs) aimed at the heterosexual population emphasize the risks men run. In a study of over three hundred PSAs in three dozen countries, nearly half did not even include women. By emphasizing the male perspective in PSAs, women are taught to believe that men are in charge of all sexual decision making. PSAs and AIDS programs in general need to begin teaching women to be independent individuals who must take responsibility for their own sex lives.

She's 48 years old with tight red curls and bags beneath her eyes. She slouches slightly in the orange office chair, stretching out her feet. From her eye shadow to her sneakers, everything she wears is blue. Married to one husband for 28 years, she has children and grandchildren. She also has AIDS. She never used drugs or had multiple sexual partners. She did have sex with her husband without a condom.

For some years now, I've been listening to women who are HIV-positive tell their stories. In support group after support group, I've heard about how they trusted their partners and how that trust was violated. The women live with an angry welter of emotions they try to repress, if only because they know the damage stress can do to their T-cell counts.

One 23-year-old had a boyfriend who had hemophilia; he never used condoms and never mentioned HIV, even though he knew he had al-

Deborah Johnson, "Women Who Trust Too Much," *On the Issues*, Summer 1996. Reprinted by permission of *On the Issues*.

ready infected another woman. A divorced man with two children didn't tell his 46-year-old girlfriend he had AIDS, not even when he was hospitalized with an AIDS-related infection. A seven-year live-in partner of another woman denied infecting her, even though he tested positive for HIV; she didn't know he was having sex outside their relationship.

All of these women discovered their HIV status only after they became seriously ill with infections they "shouldn't" have had. The numbers don't lie; heterosexual transmission in the United States is rising dramatically. Today 40 percent of newly diagnosed women become HIV-positive through heterosexual sex. In Orange County, CA, where I live, it's almost 50 percent. The seldom mentioned fact: A large percentage of these women are married or in committed relationships.

Today 40 percent of newly diagnosed women become HIV-positive through heterosexual sex.

Public education efforts around AIDS almost never deliver the message that these women needed to hear in order to protect themselves. I have analyzed more than 300 HIV/AIDS television public service announcements (PSAs) from three dozen countries as part of my doctoral dissertation research. For the most part, these educational "commercials" emphasize the risks that men—not women—run. They either ignore women entirely or offer them factual information without offering any suggestions about how to use this information in the context of casual and committed relationships.

In almost half the PSAs I studied, there were no women at all. This was true even in countries where women's infection rates equal men's. When women did appear in the PSAs, it was usually in ways that reinforced our subordinate status. The PSAs featured twice as many male as female authorities, three times as many male celebrities, and a whopping 10 times as many male narrators.

The number of women did outstrip men, however in self-effacing, care-giving roles as wives, mothers, and friends of people with AIDS. At first glance, putting women in positive roles may seem laudable. But in health education, putting a woman in *any* role is problematic. Being a wife or mother has never protected any woman from HIV/AIDS. And sex workers (as women in prostitution are called in international health promotion literature these days) who use latex condoms properly all the time are just as safe as anyone else. Showing women in these roles denies our multifaceted individuality and reduces us to only what we represent to others: a wife to a husband, a mother to a child. It strengthens long-standing notions of "good" and "bad" women. It's an easy out for PSA creators, because it makes the message seem inclusive, when in fact it is most likely exclusive.

When PSAs emphasize the risks that men, not women, run of HIV, they undercut the rights of women in relationships by positioning men as the sole sexual decision-makers. Even worse for HIV/AIDS prevention, they equate safe behavior with staying away from sex workers and being faithful to your wife. We're already experiencing their backlash, as literally thousands of women who thought themselves "safe" are finding themselves infected.

Some PSAs tried to shake middle-class women out of this complacency. But instead of striking at the heart of the problem, which is women's inclination to believe and trust men, the PSAs simply showed women in comfortable surroundings explaining how they became infected:

- GREAT BRITAIN

  Josephine had only two boyfriends. Because "we were perfectly ordinary," they didn't use condoms.

- UNITED STATES

  An African American woman with a baby didn't know "my man was shooting up drugs and sharing needles." Not until he died.

- AUSTRALIA

  Tracy never dreamed her partner had used a needle. When the doctor said she had AIDS, Tracy replied, "You've made a mistake. I can't have AIDS. How could I have that?"

PSAs like these keep women in their place. The women accept what their partners have done and, at most, regretfully shake their heads. There's no attempt to model responsible behavior for HIV-infected men. And female viewers learn nothing from them about how to ask the right questions at the right time to assess their personal risk.

When women did appear in the PSAs [public service announcements], it was usually in ways that reinforced our subordinate status.

In a handful of PSAs, women in casual relationships do broach the subject of condoms. But the scenarios are repetitive and traditional:

- AUSTRALIA

  Two pairs of feet—male and female—rub each other in bed. A woman's husky voice asks, "You've got the condoms, haven't you?"

  The man breathlessly replies, "No, I forgot."

  "But we agreed to use one," she protests.

  "I know, but I haven't got AIDS, have I?" he argues.

  Turning away, she says, "Sorry. No condom. No sex."

- UNITED STATES

  A woman in bed tells her male partner, "Don't take this the wrong way."

  The man says, "What?"

  She asks, "Do you have protection?"

  Affronted, he demands, "Do you think I'm gay?"

  "You don't have to be gay to get AIDS," she explains.

  He gets up to find a condom.

- HONG KONG

A naked couple are making love. The woman asks, "Do you have a condom?"

"Of course," he replies.

"Can I do it for you?" she offers.

None of these scenarios face up to the real difficulties. It's one thing to ask a casual partner to slip on a condom; it's quite another to ask a man who has sworn fidelity to you and been with you for years. And in both long- and short-term relationships, gender-based power imbalances can make suggesting condoms unthinkable.

Consider a woman in Peru, known to health educators, who has struggled for decades with poor eyesight. After she lost one pair of glasses, her husband refused to buy another. She was too "stupid," he said. Imagine her asking him to use condoms.

A nurse practitioner working with women on the East Coast found it was easier to help them stay off drugs than to get them to ask their partners to use condoms. If a woman did have the guts to bring up the subject, the man often refused. Some even turned abusive. Studies in Los Angeles and San Francisco found that almost half the intravenous drug–using women who are HIV-positive have experienced domestic violence.

In many cases, women fear that asking men to use condoms will lead to rejection or abandonment. If the woman is economically dependent, she and her children could wind up on the street.

Condoms also carry a stigma. Studies on every continent demonstrate that both men and women perceive condoms for use when having sex with "others," not stable partners. Or for women "of the street, not the home." Even sex workers who are scrupulous about using condoms with clients tend to avoid them with boyfriends and husbands. All too often, condom use has become a sign for the level of trust in a relationship rather than simply a sensible means of protection.

I found only one PSA in which a woman refused to use a condom:

- FRANCE

A young man explained to a male friend, "She told me that if I used condoms that would mean I didn't love her."

Today more than a million women around the world are HIV-positive. With the percentage of new cases in women skyrocketing, it's time to acknowledge that past approaches to HIV/AIDS prevention haven't worked. We need to rethink how we portray women, how we deal with gender-related power imbalances, and how we avoid the simplistic idea that if women only knew how to protect themselves, they would.

Women fear that asking men to use condoms will lead to rejection.

We could begin by creating HIV/AIDS PSAs specifically for women. These would build on the premise that women are individuals, not appendages of men and children. Separating HIV/AIDS risk from roles, the PSAs would focus on how women in *any* role communicate with partners.

Viewers don't need to know if a woman is a wife, mother, girlfriend, or sex worker. They only need to watch women express and stand up for themselves in the best ways they can.

For some women, this will mean choosing the right moment to ask a partner what he knows about HIV/AIDS. For others it will begin with a conversation about bisexuality and drug use. For still others, it may mean telling a partner they've put condoms in the nightstand. Effective communication, not sexual behavior, is the point.

PSAs can teach women to empower themselves by small steps . . . they don't have to jump to the big one right away. For example, educational messages could show how to use humor to bring up touchy subjects, how to question men in direct rather than indirect ways about their health, and how to be assertive in ways that enhance rather than threaten relationships.

Some PSAs already do this:

- SWEDEN

  A woman who wants to start using condoms playfully snaps one on her partner's bare butt. They laugh and begin talking about it.

- GERMANY

  A woman who has had sex with someone else thinks through how to tell her live-in partner that they need to use condoms.

Taking responsibility for their sex life is not easy for many women who think of sex as something that happens to them rather than something they choose. But that can change. In U.S. high schools today, teenagers are learning how to resist social pressure and stand up for what they want through practicing refusal skills, or how to say "no" without destroying their relationships. Admittedly, this is a long way from asking a husband of 28 years to start using condoms. But the underlying premise that an individual has the right to take care of herself and to communicate this to others is a new and significant shift.

Of four women I know with AIDS, two found out they were HIV-positive when they became pregnant; another casually took a free test at a class; the fourth was tested after her husband died of AIDS in jail. Not one woman's sexual partner told her that he was—or could be—HIV-positive. That has to change.

12

Society Should Continue to Stress AIDS Prevention

Michael H. Merson

Michael Merson is dean of public health at Yale University.

Although AIDS researchers are moving closer to finding a cure for the disease, it is still important to stress AIDS prevention. Even if a genuine cure is discovered, it will most likely not be accessible to the majority of AIDS victims. In addition, there is concern that strains of HIV that are resistant to the treatment might develop. AIDS prevention programs are becoming increasingly successful. Political and financial support for these programs needs to continue, regardless of the possibilities of a cure.

Early in July I took part in the 11th International Conference on AIDS. In the past, the mood at these meetings has generally been somber. But as the 15,000 participants from more than 125 countries gathered in Vancouver, there was a new spirit of optimism in the air, almost cause for celebration. For the first time, research teams were able to demonstrate real progress in the treatment of HIV infection. They showed that the daily administration of a combination of three antiretroviral drugs, costing about $15,000 a year, can clear an HIV-infected person's bloodstream of any detectable virus for at least 300 days. This news was so exciting that physicians, researchers and journalists spoke openly of a "cure" for this presumed fatal disease.

I can only express admiration for the advances made possible through biomedical research. In 15 years we've learned an enormous amount about the AIDS virus and the way it infects our white cells. This basic science has allowed rapid development, testing and licensing of these new drugs that inhibit viral replication. As someone who has seen firsthand, in scores of countries, the suffering brought about by the disease, I feel great joy that some HIV-infected persons can now live a longer life than was dreamed of two years ago.

Despite these achievements, there are still unknowns and potential long-term problems in controlling the disease. One major concern is

Michael H. Merson, "How to Fight AIDS," *Newsweek*, August 5, 1996;

whether HIV strains resistant to the new drugs will eventually develop, especially if the drugs are not taken in full dosage and on the required schedule. The three-drug regimen—as many as 20 pills a day—is daunting and can cause debilitating side effects. We've had antibiotics for treatment of gonorrhea for 50 years, but because of their inappropriate use, we have been forced repeatedly to develop new drugs to treat resistant strains. Tuberculosis has been treated with triple-drug therapy for more than 25 years, yet it is still a leading cause of death among adults worldwide and has only recently been brought under control by having health workers stand over patients at home or in clinics to make sure they take all the prescribed pills.

Another hurdle is making these costly drugs available to those who need them. This will be difficult in the United States and virtually impossible in developing countries, the home of more than 90 percent of the world's HIV-infected population. Beyond that, monitoring the level of virus in a medicated patient's blood to determine the drugs' effectiveness will be expensive.

But the most serious downside to the latest therapeutic breakthrough could be its impact on AIDS prevention. I can hear it now. If we are close to a cure, people may say, why bother with politically sensitive activities such as condom promotion, sex education in schools or disease-prevention programs for illicit drug users? Let's not invest further in trials of protective vaginal products or genetically engineered vaccines. Wouldn't the money be better spent for heart disease and cancer research?

There are still unknowns and potential long-term problems in controlling the disease.

Lost amid the excitement in Vancouver about a potential AIDS "cure" were numerous reports about prevention measures that are working in many places—from San Francisco to Bangkok to Abidjan. We heard about the success of syringe-exchange programs and learned that the failure to implement them during the past decade has led to thousands of preventable HIV infections among injecting drug users and their noninjecting (usually female) sex partners. We were told how community-based activities were resulting in safer sexual practices among inner-city women, men who have sex with men, and high-risk adolescents. There was definitive evidence that correct antibiotic treatment of common sexually transmitted diseases greatly diminishes HIV transmission. Finally, we heard about the slow but steady progress in development of an AIDS vaccine and preventive vaginal gels for women.

During the past decade, we've been able to provide more scientific evidence for the success of AIDS-prevention strategies than exists for many other diseases. Despite these achievements, political support for AIDS-prevention programs has been declining. Federal funding for AIDS prevention at the Centers for Disease Control decreased by $5 million this year. No doubt this is because the highest rates of infection have been among socially marginalized populations (gay men and drug users) and African-Americans and Latinos who lack political influence. Viewing the epidemic as a moral issue adds to the problem.

Prevention will always be a thousand times more humane and cost-effective than treatment. Since half of HIV-positive Americans are unaware they're infected, the virus will continue to be transmitted despite the availability of antiretroviral drugs. At the conference, Health and Human Services Secretary Donna Shalala pledged action for prevention programs and research. Will it result in an increase in resources and full support for programs we know are effective?

Prevention will always be a thousand times more humane and cost-effective than treatment.

Since the epidemic began, more than half a million Americans have developed AIDS; three out of five have died. AIDS is now the leading cause of death of men and women between the ages of 25 and 44 years in our country. The number of cases is increasing most rapidly among women and among those infected through heterosexual contact. Some 40,000 to 50,000 Americans are infected with HIV yearly. Half are under the age of 25. Worldwide, 8,500 people are infected daily. These numbers are unacceptable for a preventable disease.

I believe that we can now make huge inroads in treatment by widespread access to antiretroviral drugs. But equally important is political and financial support for prevention. We need to educate our youth on how to protect themselves, expand syringe-exchange programs for drug users and encourage safer sex with condoms for those at risk. Care and prevention together can save millions of lives. Then we'll have real cause for celebration.

13

Condom Distribution in Schools Will Control the Spread of AIDS

Alan Singer

Alan Singer is an assistant professor of education in the Department of Curriculum and Teaching at Hofstra University in Hempstead, New York. He is on the Board of Directors of the United Community Centers, which conducts HIV/AIDS education programs in Brooklyn under a grant from the Centers for Disease Control and Prevention.

Studies have demonstrated that many teenagers across the country are engaging in unprotected sexual intercourse. These teenagers need guidance and education. Public schools are the appropriate setting in which to teach safe sex and to distribute condoms to teenagers. Condom distribution and sex education programs, if administered properly, will not only save young lives, but will also foster responsible sexual behavior and values.

When my son was 14, he joined a program that prepared him to be a peer AIDS educator at his middle school in New York City. At several after-school workshops he learned various ways to prevent unwanted pregnancies and the spread of sexually transmitted diseases. One day, when my wife picked him up from a training session, he was holding a condom. "Here, Ma," he said. "Keep it in the glove compartment in case you need it." My wife, needless to say, was a little embarrassed.

But we are glad he got that condom. At a time when it is frequently difficult for parents to talk with teenagers, that condom opened up avenues for us to discuss AIDS and birth control with our son. The embarrassment was a small price to pay for his protection from disease and premature fatherhood.

In New York City and around the country, the controversy surrounding sex education and condom availability programs for teenagers in public high schools continues. Many parents worry that sex education and condom availability encourage increased teenage sex, but studies

Alan Singer, "Why Schools Should Make Condoms Available to Teenagers," *Educational Leadership*, vol. 52, no. 2 (October 1994), pp. 78-79. Reprinted with permission of the Association for Supervision and Curriculum Development.

across the United States repeatedly demonstrate that teenagers are already having sex at younger and younger ages without protection from pregnancy and disease.

According to the Carnegie Council on Adolescent Development, by age 16, 17 percent of girls and 29 percent of boys have had sexual intercourse. As a result, 67 percent of all births to teenagers in 1989 occurred out of wedlock (compared with 30 percent in 1970), and from 1960 to 1988, gonorrhea increased by four times among 10- to 14-year-olds.

In the November 1993 issue of *Educational Leadership*, Thomas Lickona declared that sex education and condom availability programs have failed. He called for "chastity education" to promote self-control and the "application of core ethical values" among teenagers. In the following issue, Robert Simonds, president of Citizens for Excellence in Education, presented his organization's opposition to sex education, condom availability, and other programs, describing them as "child abuse in the classroom." I want to address some of the arguments made by Lickona, Simonds, and others who oppose these programs.

The role of schools

Some opponents of sex education and condom availability programs argue that these programs violate the right of parents to educate their children about moral behavior and religious values. But as far as I know, no sex education program in the United States removes a parent or religious leader's right to teach teenagers the values that they consider to be important, including sexual abstinence. What parents and religious leaders no longer have is the right to use the public schools to impose their personal religious beliefs on their teenagers and on other people's teenage children.

Some parents, politicians, and educators have questioned whether making condoms available should be the job of the school. They argue that school should be a place for learning math and reading and science, not how to put on a condom. But public high schools are the best place to provide sex education and make condoms available to teenagers—that's where the teenagers are, and that's where there are adults who are trained and willing to counsel them. I am convinced that if teenagers openly received condoms in school instead of in bathrooms or from friends who have had them in their pockets for months, they would be more willing to use them.

Sex education and condom availability programs are an ideal way to teach responsibility for self and others.

Few educators would argue that schools should not be involved in teaching about values. Sex education and condom availability programs are an ideal way to teach responsibility for self and others, for exploring the meaning of human relationships, and for addressing "male machismo" and the lack of respect for women in our society. A sex education curriculum also helps students to understand their science lessons on human sexuality, reproduction, and the spread of disease; and to understand their social studies lessons on social relationships, the development of cultural norms, and the role of responsible citizens.

A question of character

Thomas Lickona seems particularly concerned with the development of character and with finding ways for teachers and schools to help young people examine their values and make responsible choices in their lives. With that in mind, I would like to share the words of two of my students who have shown that they can grapple with complex moral and political issues.

Until 1991, I was a high school social studies teacher in a working-class, minority New York City neighborhood and the faculty advisor to the school's Forum Club. The club brought speakers to the school to discuss controversial issues, and it organized students to be active participants in our democratic society.

Dorcas Matos represented the Forum Club at a New York City Hall rally against "parental consent laws." She told the audience:

> It was not easy for me to decide to be pro-choice. I come from a religious Hispanic family. My father is the pastor of my church. I attend church every Friday night and every Sunday morning. My father is not happy with my positions on these issues because he opposes the idea of abortion. But regardless of his personal feelings, my father has supported my right to choose my own beliefs.
>
> I believe that if I were pregnant, I would be able to get my parents' support whatever my choice. But just because I am able to talk to my parents doesn't mean that I think that informing someone's parents should be the law. . . .
>
> Often teenagers have bad relationships with their parents, and they are unable to talk with them about anything. A law that required parental consent before an abortion would not create a better relationship. It would only lead to explosions.

Novia Condell represented the Forum Club at a New York City Board of Education public hearing on condom availability in high schools. Novia told the board:

> It is certainly not a secret that many high school students are sexually active today. While some are very conscious and practice "safe sex," many do not. Many teenagers . . . deny that they can be victims of sexually transmitted diseases. They think that they are invulnerable. Condom availability in the schools, when combined with a comprehensive program of sex education, would help teenagers become more sexually responsible. This would lead to fewer teenage pregnancies and fewer sexually transmitted diseases. My advice is "Save a Life—Use a Condom!"

These young women represent the kind of thoughtful, moral high school students that Thomas Lickona and other advocates of "character education" hope to encourage. Their commitment and their knowledge empower them. They have a sense of their potential and worth as human beings; a sense of responsibility toward themselves, their peers, and their families; and an awareness of how to protect themselves from sexually transmitted diseases and unwanted pregnancies if they decide to be sexually active.

A dual responsibility

As a parent and as an educator, I agree with encouraging sexual abstinence and moral character among teenagers. But at the same time that we encourage sexual abstinence, we must also teach about sexual responsibility. And sexual responsibility today often means using a condom as a form of birth control and to prevent pregnancy and the spread of sexually transmitted diseases like AIDS.

Sex education teachers, guidance counselors, and trained peer educators should be available for counseling and to distribute condoms. Teenagers who are sexually active need to be able to get them without feeling awkward. Remember, pregnancy and disease, not abstinence, are the consequences of such embarrassment.

14

Condom Distribution in Schools Will Not Control the Spread of AIDS

Germaine O'Malley Wensley

Germaine O'Malley Wensley, a registered nurse, is a member of the Los Angeles Archdiocesan Commission on Catholic Life Issues and the former president of California Nurses for Ethical Standards.

AIDS is becoming one of the leading causes of death among teenagers and young adults. The distribution of condoms in schools, considered by some to be a solution to the crisis, actually compounds the problem by promoting promiscuous behavior. In addition, condom distribution programs are costly, and condoms' effectiveness against HIV infection is questionable. Abstinence is the only effective weapon against AIDS. Our schools need to develop abstinence-based sex education programs and begin teaching students the virtue of self-discipline.

Everyone agrees that the spread of AIDS needs to be halted, but controversy swells when we talk about how we are going to accomplish such a feat. The seriousness of the situation, however, should not dissuade us from asking ourselves the vital question: Are some of the ideas bandied about really going to help slow the deadly progress of this disease?

Since schools have ready access to our teens, there seems to be a rush to involve them in condom distribution. Apart from the morality of such a move, is it really a wise course to pursue? The choices our public agencies make in fighting the disease will have long-term effects on our entire country. For this reason, we need to look more closely at some of the moral, medical, and emotional issues involved.

In 1987, AIDS was the sixth leading cause of death among the fifteen to twenty-four-year-old population. Given the long latency period of AIDS, it could be assumed that most AIDS-infected persons now in their twenties were infected as teenagers. At the Fifth International Conference on AIDS held in 1991, it was reported that a surprising number of Amer-

Germaine O'Malley Wensley, "Condoms in the School: A Case of Educational Malpractice," *Family*, March 1993. Reprinted by permission.

ican teenagers are becoming infected with the HIV virus during early adolescence. In fact, the Centers for Disease Control statistics show that among adolescents, AIDS increased 29 percent between July 1990 and July 1991.

In response to these statistics and to pressures from many sources—including a very vocal homosexual organization called ACT-UP—one of the largest school districts in the country caved in to the condom dispensation plan. In January of 1992, despite strong parental protest, Los Angeles joined the ranks of other school districts in implementing the plan. New York, Seattle, San Francisco, Philadelphia, Columbus and several districts in Massachusetts had already voted to pass out condoms to their students.

One of the arguments used to rationalize the doling out of condoms on school property is that kids are going to have sex anyway, so they should be taught "safer sex." Several questions come to mind in response: Why are kids having sex, anyway? Who will fund the condom project? How will this affect the school atmosphere? If a child develops AIDS or any other sexually transmitted disease, or gets pregnant while using a condom provided by the school, can the school be held liable?

Let's look at the historical background leading up to the schools' promotion of condoms. Two decades ago, it was believed that schools needed to get involved in teaching kids the "facts of life." Since biology and science classes were already doing that, it really meant that the sex education or family life programs were to be broader in scope than an explanation of simple biological facts. Former U.S. Secretary of Education Dr. William Bennett was appalled to find that in sex ed courses there was "a certain pervasive tone, a certain attitude: offer students technical information, offer the facts, tell them they have choices and tell them the consequences of these choices—but do no more." Bennett went on to say, "It is a very odd kind of teaching—very odd because it does not teach! While speaking to a very important aspect of human life, it displays a conscious aversion to making moral distinctions."[1]

While strategies were being devised some twenty years ago to bring "sex ed" to the classroom, there was also a push for public funding for teen contraceptive programs. At the time there were admittedly some out-of-wedlock pregnancies, but virginity was the norm, and there were only two documented sexually transmitted diseases (STDs): syphilis and gonorrhea. Now, two decades later, we see the result of this "enlightened" educational approach: "Teenage sexual activity and teenage pregnancy have increased almost 400 percent. There are now twenty-seven documented STDs, and their rate in the sixteen to twenty-year-old age group is three times that of the population as a whole."[2]

Condom effectiveness

Aside from the serious moral issues at stake in supplying condoms to students, one might question such an action from a technical basis. For example, how effective are condoms in preventing AIDS? Medical evidence is pretty clear that trying to stop the spread of AIDS by use of condoms is fraught with danger given their unreliability, coupled with unrealistic human expectations.

Dr. Robert Noble, a specialist of infectious diseases and an AIDS doctor to the poor, has this to say about "safe sex": "Passing out condoms to teenagers is like issuing them squirt guns for a four-alarm blaze. Condoms just don't hack it. We should stop kidding ourselves."[3]

Since schools have ready access to our teens, there seems to be a rush to involve them in condom distribution.

Condoms fail to prevent pregnancy 3 to 36.3 percent of the time, depending on which study you choose to quote. It has been reported as high as 44 percent among unmarried Hispanic women. The possibility of pregnancy occurs only a few days during the average 28-day menstrual cycle—when the ovum is present to be fertilized. Infection with AIDS, however, can occur any day at any given moment, 365 days a year, with a partner infected with the HIV virus.

The FDA [Food and Drug Administration] requires 996 out of 1,000 condoms to pass a "water-leak" test. This means that as many as 1 out of every 250 condoms in a warehouse can be faulty and still pass FDA inspection! Among batches that met the minimal standard, the average failure rate was 2.3 per 1,000.[4] Even if a condom blocks sperm, it may not block viruses that are smaller than the pores of the condom's membrane.[5] Every sexual encounter while using a condom risks condom imperfection, rupture, or leakage, especially with older condoms which tend to deteriorate over time.

Some examples

Our schools are perfectly willing to tell children it is all right to rely on such flimsy protection. The tacit message given when condoms are handed out is, "It's okay to have sex—we really expect it of you—but make sure you're 'protected.'"

The following are some examples of what happens in schools where condom distribution is taking place.

In New York City, 40 percent of the condoms purchased for distribution in the schools were brands the school education program tells students *not* to use because of their high incidence of breakage.[6]

As a cost-conscious move in Florida, the Department of Health and Rehabilitation Services ordered two million condoms manufactured in Malaysia. Condoms from this order were then supplied to schools in Florida free of charge. To show the elasticity of the condoms, one of the demonstrations given in the classrooms is to stretch the condom over the lower arm. In trying this same exercise with the Malaysian condoms, a pro-family coalition found that three out of four would disintegrate.

In Philadelphia, where condom distribution was approved in June 1992, a parent advocacy group, Parents United for Better Schools (PUBS), says that the plan has created a circus-like atmosphere within the schools and is a distraction to the learning process. One teacher reported that students play with condoms on their desks; that boys blow them up, hold them to their crotch area and parade around in front of the girls. This same teacher says a boy came up to her, shook the condom in her face, and asked if he could be excused to go put on his condom. PUBS has filed a lawsuit to challenge the legality of distributing condoms in four Philadelphia schools.[7]

As a colleague and I have noted, "There is a causal relationship between the promotion of contraceptives, including condoms, and increased extramarital sexual activity. There is also a clear proportionality between the amount of extramarital sexual activity and the amount of HIV transmission. If the most dreaded risk of a pleasurable activity is promised to be reduced, then the frequency of that activity will increase. Therefore, condom promotion only serves to increase the AIDS epidemic."[8]

Teenage sexual activity and teenage pregnancy have increased almost 400 percent.

It is time to get real about what we are dealing with here. AIDS is a fatal, infectious but preventable disease, and we should begin to treat it as such. The stakes are high—but our children are too precious for us not to make the investment.

Sexually transmitted AIDS is the result of an activity that is chosen. The only sure way to avoid it is to practice sexual abstinence until marriage, to marry a person who is free of the disease, and to remain faithful to that spouse for life. Concern for morals means being concerned with the principles of right or wrong conduct and being virtuous in sexual matters. The AIDS epidemic is an area in which to practice good morals is to practice good medicine.

If a doctor prescribed a medication for a chronic, fifteen-year condition, yet the symptoms and progress of the disease steadily worsened during that time, would it make a lot of sense for that doctor to prescribe even more and larger doses of the same medicine? Would it not be wiser to change the medication?

Abstinence: The only solution

This is the situation and the choices we face in our country today. We really need to demand a stop to the moral illiteracy that has crept into our schools via "family life programs." The time is right to return to directive teaching, eliminating the wishy-washy values-clarification type of education. Our youth need to be taught unequivocally that promiscuousness is harmful to their health, and this message should not be undercut by winking and handing out condoms in the halls. To do anything less is to sell our youth short, in addition to ignoring the fact that, unlike animals, human beings can control their sexual urges. While schools teach students to say "no" to drugs and alcohol, they do not undermine this message by adding, "However, if you can't say no to the temptation, go down to see the school nurse. She has clean needles and uncontaminated drugs, and will be glad to teach you the 'safe' way to 'do drugs.'"

There are good, positive abstinence-based programs available for classroom use that give how-tos in exercising self-control, saying "no, thank you" without losing friends, and handling peer pressure while instilling a healthy respect for the beauty of sex in marriage. One side benefit of these programs is that they increase kids' self-esteem, because students feel good about themselves knowing they are in control of their own lives. The programs are cost effective, which should be especially appealing at a time when schools are crying for more money. These programs eliminate expensive school-based clinics, dramatically decrease pregnancy rates, lower the incidence of STDs, and reduce drop-out rates.

A radical overhaul of the way sex education is presented in schools is called for: giving our children the truth about condoms, AIDS, STDs; citing the dangers of premarital sex; and presenting moral absolutes. As a bare minimum, parents should have the right to choose which type of family life education their child receives. For instance, there could be two different tracks a school offers—one track giving the true abstinence message and the other a more comprehensive how-to-do "safer sex" message for parents who do not believe their children are capable of choosing abstinence. At least parents holding traditional values would not be forced into allowing their children to be exposed to teachings that undermine their family's values.

The only sure way to avoid [AIDS] is to practice sexual abstinence.

For more than twenty years, without most parents' being aware of what was happening, we have put up with educational malpractice in the area of "family life education." Proposed condom distribution in the schools has begun to stir parents to action. But this should have taken place long ago. Perhaps it is not too late to turn the tide. Let's hope not; our children's lives are depending on it.

Notes

1. Address to National School Board Association, Washington, D.C., January 22, 1987.
2. Kaye Hall, R.N., "Birth Control and Today's Teen: The Myth of Safe Sex," *LifeSupport*, Summer 1990.
3. Dr. Robert Noble, "There Is No Safe Sex," *Newsweek*, April 1, 1991, p. 8.
4. "From the Centers for Disease Control," *JAMA*, 1988.
5. Ibid.
6. Family Defense Council, *Dr. Howard Hurwitz Report*, January 1991.
7. Betty Arras, "Philadelphia Parents File Lawsuit Against Distribution of Condoms," *National Monitor of Education*, February 1992.
8. Dr. Alan Shewman and Germaine Wensley, "What Will Public Schools Teach About Sex and Sexuality?" with inclusion of letter to L.A. Unified School District from Catholic Life Issues Commission, *Tidings*, January 24, 1992. p. 11.

15

Needle-Exchange Programs Will Control the Spread of AIDS

David L. Kirp

David L. Kirp, professor of public policy at the University of California, Berkeley, is coeditor of AIDS in the Industrialized Democracies: Passions, Politics and Policies *and author of* Learning by Heart: AIDS and Schoolchildren in America's Communities.

Needle-exchange programs have been tried and tested as a possible strategy for controlling the spread of HIV infection among the intravenous drug–using population. In the past, many government officials resisted adopting such programs, fearing they would encourage drug abuse. However, research has proven such fears to be unfounded and has shown that needle-exchange programs are an effective means of controlling HIV infection among addicts. As a result, more and more communities are utilizing the programs, and lives are being saved.

At the stroke of noon on a frigid late-winter Boston day, a dozen or so shivering men and women carrying a banner announcing themselves as the AIDS Brigade began to set up shop across the street from City Hospital. They intended to hand out clean needles to intravenous drug users, they said, and immediately a handful of hopeful syringe recipients lined up. "Let us save lives," the activists demanded, but immediately they were confronted by a band of noisy antagonists. What followed wasn't exactly a discussion of the public health benefits—which are well documented—of exchanging dirty needles for clean ones to reduce the spread of HIV. "Killers!" the opponents shouted. "How many AIDS deaths will your intolerance cause?" the AIDS Brigade members countered, as a single TV camera whirred and a couple of reporters scribbled notes. Some African-American community leaders from the predominantly black neighborhood of Roxbury, who have long opposed the AIDS Brigade's tactics, were also taking notes.

Just then Jon Parker, founder of the AIDS Brigade, made his entrance. Parker was carrying cardboard boxes filled with hundreds of used, and maybe HIV-contaminated, needles that he had collected from the streets of Boston. His intention was to hand these syringes over to the city in order to embarrass public officials out of their inaction. At that moment two telegenic policemen, who had been quietly standing by, made their move. The boxes of needles were seized and stowed in the trunk of the police car, and Parker was led away, unresisting. He has been arrested dozens of times since 1986, when as a public health student at Yale he began his crusade to get clean needles into the hands of addicts.

Meanwhile, more than a hundred needle-exchange advocates were convening for the North American Syringe Exchange Convention across town at the Government Center Holiday Inn. The talks were studded with street-smart colloquialisms and drug lingo. Clusters of syringes were pinned on lapels as ersatz boutonnieres; tie-dye and jeans were the sartorial order of the day. The session's organizer, Dave Purchase, who effectively launched the needle exchange movement in 1988 when he set up a TV tray on the streets of Tacoma, Washington, looked like a shambling bear. Cigarette smoke hung thick in the anteroom adjacent to the meeting hall, mute testimony to the fact that addictions can be hard to beat.

More states pick up needle exchange programs

Yet for all its countercultural style, the Boston gathering signaled something very mainstream: Needle exchange has come of age politically. The research to back this approach to AIDS prevention has been accumulating for some time. In the late 1980s, studies from several locales—notably Amsterdam, Sydney, Edinburgh and southern Sweden—showed markedly lower increases in HIV infection rates among addicts who exchanged dirty syringes for clean ones. In 1991, confirming research was reported in Tacoma, the first American city to adopt such a program, and in New Haven, where Yale University scientists have been conducting perhaps the most analytically sophisticated efficacy study. The research has rebutted narcotics officials' fears that such a venture would encourage people to try heroin.

Now other American communities are getting the message. Between 1990 and 1993 the estimated number of I.V. [intravenous] needles swapped in the United States more than tripled, to nearly 4 million annually. An impressive array of locales that operate, or at least tolerate, exchange programs sent representatives to Boston, among them New York City, the epicenter of the drugs/AIDS pandemic; New Haven; Philadelphia; Chicago; Seattle; San Francisco; Hawaii (where a statewide program is running); and smaller cities and rural outposts like Boulder, Colorado, and Wyndham, Connecticut.

There were dispirited accounts from Providence and Rochester, where activists have unsuccessfully tried to launch programs; but the feeling was that in these cities, success was just a matter of time. And although there were tales of failures from places like Indianapolis, where the one-man underground operation run by a renegade Public Health Department employee is out of funds, these were the conspicuous exceptions.

Jon Parker made an appearance at the convention the morning after his arrest, but the featured speaker was a quintessentially establishment figure, Dr. Jonathan Mann, who during the 1980s ran the World Health Organization's much-praised AIDS initiative. Mann is now the François-Xavier Bagnoud Professor of Public Health at Harvard.

Several legislators threw a reception for the group at Doric Hall in the Massachusetts State House. Boston Mayor Ray Flynn added his welcoming words: "As you know, Boston has been a national leader in the effort to . . . remove the legal barriers that prevent [drug users'] access to clean needles. . . . In 1987, our early efforts led Boston to become the first city in the United States to approve the development of a needle/syringe exchange program."

In most of the industrialized world, clean needles are as readily available as aspirin.

Yet the Mayor added that needle exchange remains illegal in Boston, since the Massachusetts law that prohibits the possession of hypodermic needles without a prescription is still on the books. When legalization was first proposed, in the midst of Michael Dukakis's run for the presidency, the Governor wasn't about to endorse this kind of social experimentation, so the idea died. Half a decade later, it's only at Parker-orchestrated performances—and in the far more effective efforts quietly being made by a group that calls itself the I.V. League—that syringes are being swapped in Boston.

But 1993 looked like a watershed year for needle exchange. With new political backers, including Republican Governor William Weld and black community leaders, syringe exchange will probably be authorized in the Bay State. Elsewhere, notably in California and Pennsylvania, conservative governors are coming under renewed pressure to legalize needle exchange. The Mayor of San Francisco, himself a former police chief, is defying the Governor's edicts; he has announced a public health state of emergency and is backing up his words with city money for syringes. Within the Clinton Administration there is support for this public health initiative, and that too represents a major shift.

During the late 1980s, when almost no American politician would take needle exchange seriously—and when many powerful black leaders were savaging the idea as a genocidal plot aimed at African-Americans—confrontation seemed the only way to get anyone to pay attention. But that time has passed. Parker's public performances convince no one anymore; they just stiffen the opposition's resolve. The real reason change is occurring is that, both in government offices and in the trenches, the parties involved are talking to, rather than past, one another.

This shift in mood was evident at the Boston convention, where one remarkable session brought together the leading players in that city's drama. "I remember that in the 1970s we were going to be saved by methadone," said Ellarwee Gadsen from Women, Inc., which helps addicts kick the habit. Gadsen was one of those taking notes at Parker's street scene. "We were going to rescue addicts and the inner city. But when the money was withdrawn, the methadone stayed but the help was gone." Gadsen acknowledged that needle exchange was likely to occur, but she was pushing for a program that guaranteed not just a syringe but drug treatment to anyone who wanted it. "In the year 2000, I don't want to see a dispensing machine for condoms and needles."

Pedro Muñoz, an AIDS activist on the other side of the issue, had his own memories to recite. "I remember going to pediatric AIDS wards and seeing all those children. I remember going to too many funerals of people who have died from AIDS." Blacks and Latinos had to help themselves, Muñoz added, making a point that drew general concurrence. "When Jon Parker walked into our community and told us, 'This is what you need,' he totally disrespected people of color."

Such a public give-and-take could never have happened a year earlier. Then, Boston's ethnic leaders seemed hopelessly divided, and the splits played into the hands of opponents. But many of these convention panelists had been quietly meeting for months to hammer out a compromise on needle exchange. Initially, advocates of exchange like the I.V. League insisted that the only "community" they acknowledged was the community of drug users. For their part, treatment proponents like Ellarwee Gadsen and Lawrence Robinson were fearful that needle exchanges would be boosted as a quick, cheap fix. "AIDS groups don't realize that in the minority community, AIDS is not the biggest concern; drugs and crime are the real focus," says Robinson. Yet over time, these opponents began to be swayed by the data from New Haven—and by the frank recognition that, since something was likely to happen, they were better off having a role in the new venture than merely nay-saying. They signed off on a set of guiding principles, among them that drug treatment had to be part of the package and that any affected neighborhood was entitled to participate in deciding how the exchange program would be run.

It's the right moment . . . to pronounce this syringe-exchange experiment a success and get on with implementing a program of delivering clean needles.

The core principle is as profound as it is obvious. As Dr. Alonzo Plough, the city Health Department official who has patiently kept the old antagonists talking to one another, said, "The point is to save lives." Rhoda Creamer from Project Trust, which does HIV testing, made the same point more graphically: "We're all talking up here. I see a casket down there." In most of the industrialized world, clean needles are as readily available as aspirin—part of a broader public health initiative to lessen the harm done by AIDS and drugs. By not endorsing needle exchange, the United States has fallen behind in this aspect of the international war on AIDS.

The events in Boston, both at the convention and in the behind-the-scenes political negotiations, suggest that it is time for a new strategy. It's the right moment, as a matter of policy and politics, for the United States to pronounce this syringe-exchange experiment a success and get on with implementing a program of delivering clean needles—and treatment—on demand.

16

Needle-Exchange Programs Will Not Control the Spread of AIDS

Mitchell S. Rosenthal

Mitchell S. Rosenthal, president of Phoenix House, a drug rehabilitation agency, is chairman of the New York State Advisory Council on Substance Abuse.

Despite media reports of their success, needle-exchange programs have yet to be proven as an effective means for reducing HIV infection among addicts. The supporting research is based on questionable assumptions and is therefore inconclusive. However, even if needle exchange prevented the sharing of needles, it would do nothing to control the spread of HIV from addicts to their sexual partners via unsafe sex. Addicts engage in this type of sexual behavior due to their general inability or unwillingness to accept responsibility. Drug addicts need treatment—not clean needles—in order to become productive, responsible citizens.

Allowing drug users to exchange dirty needles for new ones seems like an enlightened idea—simple, sensible and compassionate. AIDS is rampant among addicts who inject heroin or cocaine, and they transmit the HIV virus to one another by sharing needles and syringes.

No evidence of success

But despite all the happy headlines and editorials, there is no evidence that this approach actually works and will reduce transmission of the virus.

Let's look at the widely reported "success" of a model needle-exchange program in New Haven. A preliminary report predicted a 33 percent reduction in new infections among addicts in the program. But this result was projected, not achieved. Using a mathematical model, the report forecast, after seven months, what the program would accomplish in a year.

Mitchell S. Rosenthal, "Giving Away Needles Won't Stop AIDS," *New York Times*, August 17, 1991.

Mathematical models cannot produce valid results unless all the information they include is accurate. The New Haven model makes several questionable assumptions, and the key issue—how needle-sharing behavior has changed—is not addressed directly.

Instead, the returned needles are tracked and tested. When a participant in the program returns someone else's needles, the conclusion is that those needles were shared. But when an addict returns the same needles he or she was issued, it is assumed that the needles were *not* used by anyone else.

> *AIDS is being spread most rapidly by heterosexual contact, primarily through transmission of the virus from intravenous drug users to their sexual partners.*

Even if it were possible to discover by this means which needles were shared, it would not reveal how many intravenous drug users were sharing them. By testing, it is possible to discover how many needles are contaminated with the HIV virus, but not how many intravenous drug users have been exposed. Casting further doubt on the New Haven projection is the apparent failure to consider how the high dropout rate—60 percent—might skew the findings.

But premature optimism has put opponents of needle exchange on the defensive, and revealing the study's flaws isn't likely to reduce the pressure for more such programs. Even if it doesn't work, supporters demand, what's the harm in trying? It isn't enough to argue that needle exchange puts government in the bizarre position of abetting illegal and life-threatening behavior that we have been trying desperately to control.

But we can point out that clean needles, even if they could prevent sharing, wouldn't reduce a spread of the AIDS virus from addicts to people who don't use drugs. In the U.S. today, AIDS is being spread most rapidly by heterosexual contact, primarily through transmission of the virus from intravenous drug users to their sexual partners. Clean needles won't alter irresponsible sexual behavior.

Indeed, clean needles aren't going to alter any of the irresponsible and antisocial ways in which drug abusers threaten society. Only treatment can do this. And although clean-needle programs may provide a route to treatment for some drug users, the overwhelming effect would be to impede their movement into treatment.

To be effective, treatment must make demands of drug abusers that few are willing to accept. The great majority will only enter treatment under pressure—and pressure on addicts directly reflects public attitudes about drugs.

By accommodating drug use, through needle exchange, we foster ambivalence, making it harder for communities to discourage drug use and demand that abusers accept treatment.

When we consider this cost and the absence of any proven benefits, we might question whether needle exchange is really such a terrific idea.

Organizations to Contact

The editors have compiled the following list of organizations concerned with the issues debated in this book. The descriptions are derived from materials provided by the organizations themselves. All have publications or information available for interested readers. The list was compiled on the date of publication of the present volume; names, addresses, phone and fax numbers, and e-mail/internet addresses may change. Be aware that many organizations take several weeks or longer to respond to inquiries, so allow as much time as possible.

Adolescent AIDS Program
Montefiore Medical Center
111 E. 210th St.
Bronx, NY 10467
(718) 882-0023
fax: (718) 882-0432

The Adolescent AIDS Program opened in 1987 as the first program to provide medical and psychosocial care to HIV-positive and at-risk adolescents aged 13–21. It also conducts research and provides education for health professionals and students about AIDS and adolescents. The program has many position papers available concerning AIDS, including "Teens and AIDS: Identifying and Testing Those at Risk" and "Treating HIV-Positive Adolescents."

AIDS Coalition to Unleash Power (ACT UP)
332 Bleecker St., Suite G5
New York, NY 10014
(212) 642-5499
fax: (212) 642-5499
e-mail: ACTUPNY@Panix.com

ACT UP is composed of individuals committed to ending AIDS. Its members believe that politicians, doctors, and researchers are not doing enough to combat the disease. To improve public awareness of AIDS, ACT UP members meet with government officials, hold protests, distribute medical information, and publish various materials, including the handbook *Women and AIDS*.

AIDS National Interfaith Network (ANIN)
110 Maryland Ave. NE, Suite 504
Washington, DC 20002
(202) 546-0807
fax: (202) 546-5103

The ANIN is a coalition of religious organizations whose goal is to see that everyone affected by AIDS receives compassion, respect, care, and assistance. The network opposes threats to the civil liberties of AIDS patients, including violations of confidentiality and all forms of prejudice and discrimination.

Among the organization's publications are the handbooks *America Living with AIDS* and *AIDS and Your Religious Community*.

American Civil Liberties Union (ACLU)
132 W. 43rd St.
New York, NY 10036
(212) 944-9800
fax: (212) 869-9065
web site: http://www.aclu.org

The ACLU champions the rights set forth in the Declaration of Independence and the U.S. Constitution. It opposes any actions, including testing and contact tracing, that might endanger the civil rights of people with AIDS. The ACLU's numerous publications include the book *The Rights of Lesbians and Gay Men*, which contains a section on discrimination against people with AIDS, and the briefing paper "AIDS and Civil Liberties."

Family Research Council (FRC)
700 13th St. NW, Suite 500
Washington, DC 20005
(202) 393-2100
fax: (202) 393-2134
web site: http://www.frc.org

The FRC believes in strengthening the institutions of marriage and the family. It considers AIDS to be part of a larger, broader social problem that can be combatted through promoting primary prevention methods, such as sexual abstinence until marriage and monogamy within marriage. The FRC publishes various position papers regarding AIDS policy, including "The Social Impact of the AIDS Lobby," "How to Overhaul AIDS Spending," and "Will Needle Exchange Save America's Future?"

Focus on the Family
8605 Explorer Dr.
Colorado Springs, CO 80920
(719) 531-3400
fax: (719) 531-3331

Focus on the Family is a Christian organization that seeks to strengthen the traditional family in America. It promotes abstinence from sex until marriage as a way for teenagers to avoid AIDS, and it advocates monogamy within marriage. It publishes a number of materials, including the booklet *AIDS: Facts vs. Fiction*, the information sheet "AIDS Resources," and the monthly magazine *Focus on the Family*.

Gay Men's Health Crisis (GMHC)
129 W. 20th St.
New York, NY 10011-0022
(212) 807-6655
fax: (212) 337-3656

The GMHC, founded in 1982, is the oldest and largest AIDS network. It provides support services, education, and advocacy for men, women, and children with AIDS. The group publishes the monthly AIDS therapy journal *Treat-*

ment Issues as well as a variety of position papers.

The Hetrick-Martin Institute (HMI)
2 Astor Pl.
New York, NY 10003
(212) 674-2400
fax: (212) 674-8650

The HMI offers a broad range of social services to gay and lesbian adolescents and their families as well as to all teenagers at high risk of AIDS. It provides direct services to gay and lesbian youth, including group and individual counseling and referral, outreach services to homeless youth, and education on human sexuality and AIDS. The HMI publishes the quarterly newsletter *HMI Report Card.*

Mothers' Voices
165 W. 46th St., Suite 1310
New York, NY 10036
(212) 730-2777
fax: (212) 730-4378

Mothers' Voices is composed of mothers concerned about AIDS. It works for AIDS education to prevent the transmission of HIV, the promotion of safer sexual behavior, research for better treatments and a cure, and compassion for every person living with HIV and AIDS. The group publishes the newsletter *Speaking from the Heart* three times a year and the policy statement *Expanded Bio-Medical Research.*

National AIDS Fund
1400 I St. NW, Suite 1220
Washington, DC 20005-2208
(202) 408-4848
fax: (202) 408-1818

The fund is dedicated to eliminating HIV as a major health and social problem. It works with the public and private sectors to provide care and prevent new infections through advocacy, grant-making, research, and education in communities and the workplace. The fund's numerous publications include the booklet *The ADA, FMLA, and AIDS: An Employer's Guide to Managing HIV-Infected Employees* and *A Generation at Risk: A Background Report on HIV Prevention and Youth.*

The Rockford Institute
934 N. Main St.
Rockford, IL 61103
(815) 964-5053
fax: (815) 965-1826

The institute calls for rebuilding moral values and recovering the traditional American family. It believes that AIDS is a symptom of the decline of the traditional family and that only by supporting traditional families and traditional moral behavior will America rid itself of AIDS. The institute publishes the monthlies *Chronicles, Family in America,* and *Religion & Society Report.*

Bibliography

Books

Elinor Burkett	*The Gravest Show on Earth: America in the Age of AIDS.* Boston: Houghton Mifflin, 1995.
Miriam E. Cameron	*Living with AIDS, Experiencing Ethical Problems.* Newbury Park, CA: Sage, 1993.
Ralph J. DiClemente, ed.	*Adolescents and AIDS: A Generation in Jeopardy.* Newbury Park, CA: Sage, 1992.
Ralph J. DiClemente and John L. Peterson, eds.	*Preventing AIDS: Theories and Methods of Behavioral Interventions.* New York: Plenum, 1994.
Timothy Edgar, Mary Anne Fitzpatrick, and Vicki S. Freimuth, eds.	*AIDS: A Communication Perspective.* Hillsdale, NJ: Lawrence Erlbaum Associates, 1992.
M. Daniel Fernando	*AIDS and Intravenous Drug Use: The Influence of Morality, Politics, Social Science, and Race in the Making of a Tragedy.* Westport, CT: Praeger, 1993.
Mary Fisher	*I'll Not Go Quietly: Mary Fisher Speaks Out.* New York: Scribner, 1995.
Michael Fumento	*The Myth of Heterosexual AIDS.* New York: Basic Books, 1990.
Robin Gorna	*Vamps, Virgins, and Victims: How Can Women Fight AIDS?* London: Cassell, 1996.
Christine Grady	*The Search for an AIDS Vaccine: Ethical Issues in the Development and Testing of a Preventive HIV Vaccine.* Bloomington: Indiana University Press, 1995.
Jeffrey A. Kelly	*Changing HIV Risk Behavior: Practical Strategies.* New York: Guilford Publications, 1995.
Edward King	*Safety in Numbers: Safer Sex and Gay Men.* London: Cassell, 1993.
Judith Landau-Stanton and Coleen D. Clements and Associates	*AIDS, Health, and Mental Health: A Primary Sourcebook.* New York: Brunner/Mazel, 1993.
Ann O'Leary	*Women at Risk: Issues in the Primary Prevention of AIDS.* New York: Plenum, 1995.
Kenneth R. Overberg, ed.	*AIDS, Ethics, and Religion: Embracing a World of Suffering.* Maryknoll, NY: Orbis Books, 1995.
Cindy Patton	*Fatal Advice: How Safe-Sex Education Went Wrong.* Durham, NC: Duke University Press, 1996.

Tomas J. Philipson and Richard A. Posner — *Private Choices and Public Health: The AIDS Epidemic in an Economic Perspective.* Cambridge, MA: Harvard University Press, 1993.

B. D. Schoub — *AIDS and HIV in Perspective: A Guide to Understanding the Virus and Its Consequences.* New York: Cambridge University Press, 1994.

Robert S. Walker — *AIDS Today, Tomorrow: An Introduction to the HIV Epidemic in America.* Atlantic Highlands, NJ: Humanities Press International, 1994.

Periodicals

Addresses are provided for periodicals not indexed in the *Social Science Index*, the *Alternative Press Index*, the *Readers' Guide to Periodical Literature*, or the *Index to Legal Periodicals & Books*.

Peter Aggleton, Kevin O'Reilly, and Gary Slutkin — "Risking Everything? Risk Behavior, Behavior Change, and AIDS," *Science*, July 15, 1994.

Lawrence K. Altman — "AIDS Cases Increase Among Heterosexuals," *New York Times*, March 11, 1994.

Ricky Bluthenthal — "Combating the AIDS Pandemic," *CrossRoads*, November 1995.

Alan D. Bowd and Cynthia H. Loos — "Gender Differences in Adoption of AIDS Preventive Behaviors: Implications for Women's AIDS Education Programs," *Women's Health Issues*, Spring 1995. Available from Journals Fulfillment Department, Elsevier Science, Inc., 655 Avenue of the Americas, New York, NY 10010.

Sandy Carter — "The Fight Against AIDS: An Interview with John Iversen," *Z Magazine*, May 1995.

Amitai Etzioni — "HIV Sufferers Have a Responsibility," *Time*, December 13, 1993.

Futurist — "Innovative AIDS Programs," January/February 1994.

Robin Henig — "The Lessons of Syphilis in the Age of AIDS," *Civilization*, November/December 1995. Available from PO Box 420235, Palm Coast, FL 32142-0235.

Deborah Holtzman and Richard Rubinson — "Parent and Peer Communication Effects on AIDS-Related Behavior Among U.S. High School Students," *Family Planning Perspectives*, November/December 1995. Available from Circulation Manager, 111 Fifth Ave., New York, NY 10003.

Don C. des Jarlais, Nancy S. Padian, and Warren Winkelstein Jr. — "Targeted HIV-Prevention Programs," *New England Journal of Medicine*, November 24, 1994. Available from 10 Shattuck Street, Boston, MA 02115-6094.

Anne M. Johnson — "Condoms and HIV Transmission," *New England Journal of Medicine*, August 11, 1994.

Gina Kolata — "New Picture of Who Will Get AIDS Is Crammed with Addicts," *New York Times*, February 28, 1995.

Barbara Leigh et al.	"Not at Risk," *Family in America*, January 1994. Available from PO Box 416, Mt. Morris, IL 61054.
Charles Marwick	"Released Report Says Needle Exchanges Work," *JAMA*, April 5, 1995. Available from the American Medical Association, PO Box 10945, Chicago, IL 60610.
Michael H. Merson	"Slowing the Spread of HIV: Agenda for the 1990s," *Science*, May 28, 1993.
John Michelena Jr.	"Why the Opposition to AIDS Contact Tracing?" *USA Today*, January 1995.
Susan Moran	"Stopping the Flow of Tainted Blood," *Insight*, August 2, 1993. Available from PO Box 96067, Washington, DC 20090-6067.
Martina Morris, Jane Zavisca, and Laura Dean	"Social and Sexual Networks: Their Role in the Spread of HIV/AIDS Among Young Gay Men," *AIDS Education and Prevention*, vol. 7, Supplement, 1995. Available from Guilford Publications, 72 Spring St., New York, NY 10012.
Shawn Neidorf	"The Damage Done," *In These Times*, August 8–21, 1994.
Walt Odets	"The Fatal Mistakes of AIDS Education," *Harper's Magazine*, May 1995.
David E. Rogers and June E. Osborn	"AIDS Policy: Two Divisive Issues," *JAMA*, July 28, 1993.
Steve Salerno	"AIDS: Undue Alarm," *American Legion*, September 1993. Available from 5561 W. 74th St., Indianapolis, IN 46268.
Philip Shenon	"AIDS Epidemic, Late to Arrive, Now Explodes in Populous Asia," *New York Times*, January 21, 1996.
SIECUS Report	Issue on "HIV/AIDS: Next Steps in Prevention Education," December 1994/January 1995. Available from 130 W. 42nd St., Suite 2500, New York, NY 10036.
Helen Mathews Smith	"AIDS: Civil Liberties vs. Lives," *Wall Street Journal*, September 13, 1994.
Rebecca M. Turner	"AIDS Threat Leads Some U.S. Women to Change Their Sexual Behavior," *Family Planning Perspectives*, March/April 1994.
Rebecca M. Turner	"Condom Use Is Low Among U.S. Heterosexuals at Risk of HIV Infection; 15% of Population Has at Least One Risk Factor," *Family Planning Perspectives*, January/February 1993.
Isabelle de Vincenzi	"A Longitudinal Study of Human Immunodeficiency Virus Transmission by Heterosexual Partners," *New England Journal of Medicine*, August 11, 1994.
Rebecca Voelker	"Foes of Mandatory Maternal HIV Testing Fear Guidelines Will Lead to Reprisals," *JAMA*, April 5, 1995.
Philip Yam	"Dangerous Sex," *Scientific American*, February 1995.

Index